THE ANGLERS
COOKBOOK
FROM HOOK TO TABLE BY VIC DUNAWAY

FS Books:

Sport Fish of Florida
Sport Fish of the Gulf of Mexico
Sport Fish of the Atlantic
Sport Fish of Fresh Water
Sport Fish of the Pacific

Baits, Rigs & Tackle
Sportsman's Best: Snapper & Grouper
Sportsman's Best: Inshore Fishing
Sportsman's Best: Sailfish
Sportsman's Best: Offshore Fishing
Sportsman's Best: Redfish

Annual Fishing Planner

Florida Sportsman Magazine
Shallow Water Angler Magazine
Florida Sportsman Fishing Charts
Lawsticks
Law Boatstickers

Recipe photos by the author

Fried fish cover photo setting:
Prawnbroker Restaurant, Stuart, FL

Art Direction: Drew Wickstrom

Graphics Support: Jim Henderson

Edited by Joe Richard

Copy Editor: Jerry McBride

By Vic Dunaway

www.floridasportsman.com/books

CONTENTS

A nice mutton snapper destined
for the dinner table. A number of
snapper species remain extremely
popular with seafood lovers.

FOREWORD

For uncounted millions of recreational anglers, the catch of a potentially delectable fish immediately poses some big questions: How good is this fish to eat? How should it be cooked? What's the best way to clean it?

The Anglers Cookbook answers those questions, and many more, handsomely and in depth.

The timing for this valuable new reference is perfect because never before has there been so much interest in the healthful qualities of fish, that not only provide an excellent source of low-fat protein, but also some essential nutrients that are scarce in most other foods. And, of course, the many varieties of freshwater and saltwater fish that abound in North American waters offer an endless array of tantalizing table prospects.

Proper recipe selection and preparation take on even more importance in the modern age of sports angling, when more and more fish are being released to fight again. The comparatively few that are brought home to grace the sportsman's table are looked upon as special culinary treats deserving of the angler-cook's utmost attention.

But even though catch-and-release is standard practice today among many sports anglers, that doesn't mean they have to surrender the pleasure of a fresh fish dinner. Even heavily pressured species that benefit most from catch-and-release (like bass or trout in fresh water and striped bass or redfish in salt water) can be eaten without concern, when taken in compliance with the strict regulations that now prevail in all jurisdictions.

Happier still for all who love fish on the table is the fact that many of our most delicious species are prolific breeders that can easily withstand substantial harvesting and, consequently, carry quite liberal catch allowances, and for some, no limits at all. These include, but are by no means limited to, perch, crappie, bluegill, catfish and many small but sporty saltwater types.

Although *The Anglers Cookbook* offers more than 100 tantalizing recipes, author Vic Dunaway devotes no less attention to the important details involved in the basic methods of fish preparation—baking, broiling, sautéing, frying, poaching, stewing, grilling, smoking. Just plain good eatin', if you will.

So land that fish and enjoy!

Karl Wickstrom

INTRODUCTION

It's an all too common lament:"I just can't cook fish."

Maybe you've heard it yourself. Maybe you've said it yourself. If so, don't give up yet. Chances are you can pin past failures on just one simple error—overcooking.

Unlike other meats, which often become more tender with longer cooking, fish just gets drier, and usually tougher. Serve up your fish while it's flaky and juicy and you'll get compliments, not complaints.

No matter whether you're serving plain fried fish or one of the more elaborate fish recipes in the pages that follow, it's important to master the basic cooking methods, and always with the cardinal rule in mind: Don't overcook.

For millions of sportsmen and sportswomen who catch most of the fish that grace their tables (or try to, anyway), this book will make cooking them easier than it's ever been before. And the eating part even more enjoyable.

Perhaps no other food is so dependent on freshness for optimum enjoyment as fish. Beef and some other types of red meat may be improved by aging—that is, by deliberately allowing the carcass, under controlled conditions, to develop a flavor, which is "riper" than that of fresh meat. But with fish, the aim always is to maintain that delicate, fresh-caught taste, and to prevent even the slightest hint of "ripeness." Many kinds of fish, if properly frozen, can be eaten months after they are caught and still taste perfectly fresh. Yet the very same kinds might just as easily develop a disagreeably strong flavor only a day—even hours—after being pulled from the water. The difference, of course, lies in how well they are cared for and cold-stored.

As for the "right" way to cook each individual species, there isn't any! If the angler simply follows the few simple procedures explained here for the various methods of cooking, he'll have little trouble making a tasty dish out of any fish he might catch.

Nearly all kinds of edible fish can be tastily prepared by any cooking method you might prefer. But it's also true that certain kinds may be better suited to one method than to another. For that reason, we have included in this volume a comprehensive, illustrated guide that enables the reader to recognize the fish he has in hand and to find suggestions as to its table qualities and best cooking methods. The guide covers *most* of the popular sport and food fish of North America, whether from fresh water or from the coast.

If you're puzzled about your fish, the best way to proceed is to first look it up in chapter 11. Then, allow the suggestions on how best to dress and cook to it lead you to appropriate instructions and recipes in the other chapters. Almost always there is a wide choice of possibilities for any food fish. Once you decide on a preference, you'll find everything you need to know right here.

It always pays, to check for any health advisories that affect local areas. Such advisories are necessary because of man-made pollutants that plague particular waters, and most of them simply advise limiting the quantity and frequency for eating specified types of fish. Because they vary so widely around the country, it is impossible to compile a complete list of such warnings in this or any other book, but they can easily be referenced through local fishery agencies and health departments.

FISH in the SKILLET
Deep-Frying, Pan-Frying, Sautéing

Fried fish is the traditional favorite of most anglers—carbohydrates, calories and cholesterol notwithstanding.   Fortunately, all three of those villains can be greatly reduced, without greatly reducing the appeal of your fish. Calories and cholesterol stay within at least modest bounds when you substitute light vegetable oils for the lard or solid shortening that was favored by past generations. As for carbs, they lurk mostly in the coating and can be defeated by simply sautéing your fish in olive oil or butter, instead of breading them.

DEEP-FRYING

Deep-fried fish nearly always wears a coating, and the reason is plain to see—and to smell. When coated and properly fried, your fish will turn out brown and crisp on the outside, flaky and moist on the inside, and scrumptiously aromatic.

For successful fish frying, the keys are time and temperature, and if you get the temperature right, the timing will often take care of itself.

You must not only achieve the right temperature but maintain it. Because of this, you should always use either a cast iron pan or heavy-gauge aluminum. There are other options, such as cast iron Dutch ovens, electric deep-fryers and large, gas-fired cookers.

The best frying temperature for whole panfish or thick fillets and steaks is usually around 350 degrees, but you might go as high as 375 degrees for thin fillets. The majority of fillets run less than a half-inch thick, and 375 is ideal for those.

When frying in a pan, it's a good idea to use a frying thermometer. If you proceed by instinct, the right burner setting is usually medium to medium-high. By using the same equipment on the same stove, a little trial-and-error will show the proper setting.

First, test-fry one piece of fish. It should sizzle as soon as it hits the oil, and brown on one side in not much more than a minute. I like to turn the fish once and brown the other side equally.

Electric and gas cookers generally include baskets that allow you to lower several pieces of breaded fish into the oil at once. If you batter your fish, however, be sure to drop the pieces directly into the oil, one at a time. You can still use the basket to raise and drain pieces after cooking.

Fish for frying should not be cut thicker than about a half-inch. Any thicker and the frying time will have to be increased while the heat is sharply lowered to prevent browning too quickly. There should be ample oil in the pan to cover.

Unless you have a wire basket, the most useful implement for frying is a long-handled, slotted spoon. Remove pieces one or two at a dip, let them drip a moment, and then drop the pieces on absorbent paper.

1 First step is to slice the fish in thin strips (called fingers), which makes them cook more quickly and evenly. Moisten lightly with water.

2 Roll each dampened piece thoroughly in flour or cornmeal. Many cooks are fond of adding in a good shaking of Cajun spice, which includes red pepper. The spice certainly helps with the flavor.

3 Mix 2 eggs and milk (approximately 1 cup) in a bowl. Mustard and beer added in are optional. Dip flour-coated fish in the mixture.

Coat fish in crushed `4`
Saltine crackers, cereal or
light-colored bread
crumbs. Set aside for 15
minutes before frying to
help coating stick to fish.

Drop pieces (gently) into `5`
hot oil. They should boil
instantly, or the oil isn't
hot enough. If the oil
smokes, it's too hot and
will overcook. Keep oil
ideally at 375 degrees for
the very best results.

Don't get distracted and `6`
allow fish to overcook.
When they're a light
brown, remove a piece
and see if it flakes easily,
then remove the rest.
Allow to cool on folded
paper towels.

Frying fish for a large group needn't be intimidating. With proper planning, little enough trouble is involved—provided, that others take care of the rest and let you stick to the frying. Figure the amount of fish required as follows:

Fillets—one quarter pound per person
Steaks—one half pound per person
Panfish—one pound per person

Add a couple of pounds "for the pot" if you want to play it safe, but those figures are surprisingly accurate.

If cooking at a remote site, make most of your preparations at home. Cut the fish into serving-size pieces and salt it. Then pack it in plastic containers for temporary holding in a portable cooler. Hush puppies also should be mixed in advance.

Your challenge is to turn out quantities of fish, fast enough for all the guests to enjoy while it's piping hot. To do this, you must bring your cooking oil to the appropriate high temperature, keep it there throughout the cooking, and set up an efficient operating system.

As soon as you arrive at the site, fire up the stove. A large, bottled-gas deep-fryer, available from many sporting goods stores, is by far the most efficient gear for quantity cooking. While the oil heats in your cooker, bread the fish pieces and remove them to a tray. Continue until all the fish is breaded.

Place your tray of fish, the hush puppy mix and take-up pans within easy reach. .

Drop pieces of fish gently into the cooker, until a comfortable capacity is reached. As the first pieces turn an appetizing brown or gold, remove them with the draining basket (or a slotted spoon) and add others.

Very shortly, you should reach the point where you are constantly dipping up some of the pieces and replacing them.

From time to time, hold up on new fish and, instead, drop six or eight hush puppies into the pan with a tablespoon. This will keep both of them going at once so the chow line can begin to form right away.

FISH FRIED IN CORN MEAL

- ✔ **Thin fillets or small whole fish**
- ✔ **Buttermilk or milk**
- ✔ **2 parts corn meal**
- ✔ **1 part flour**
- ✔ **Salt and pepper**
- ✔ **Garlic powder (optional)**

This is the simplest and most common procedure for deep-frying, but take note that meal-based coatings generally do not brown as quickly as a crumb or instant potato coating; therefore, it's best to use the highest temperature that is consistent with the thickness of your fish. Try to keep the fillets rather thin and the temperature rather high, about 375 degrees.

1 Soak the fish for an hour or more in buttermilk or milk (mix in beer, egg and mustard if you wish). If in a hurry, simply wet fish thoroughly with water.

2 Sprinkle the wet fish with salt, pepper and garlic powder to your taste (to most fish-lovers who are not on a diet, this means "liberally"). Coat fish thoroughly by shaking in a bag or a lidded plastic container containing the meal mixture.

Self-rising corn meal may be substituted for the mix listed above. Or you might prefer to use one of the many meal-based, ready-seasoned coatings you find in catalogs or on your grocer's shelf.

HUSH PUPPIES

- ✔ 1 cup self-rising corn meal
- ✔ 1 small onion, grated or finely chopped
- ✔ one egg, beaten lightly
- ✔ ⅓ cup milk or tomato juice

Fish and hush puppies are the American answer to fish and chips, especially in the South. Hush puppies are mixed in advance and fried along with the fish, at the same temperature and in jig time. Tomato or V8 juice substituted for the milk adds a rosy color to the hush puppies. Actually, any liquid can be substituted, whether beer, cola, or even plain water.

1 Measure the meal into a small bowl and grate the onion directly into it. Add egg. Add milk or juice slowly, stirring until the batter is moist, yet stiff enough to hold shape when formed or when dropped from a spoon.

For looks you can form each hush puppy by hand into the shape of a tiny football. It's faster, however, simply to drop them by the half-tablespoon directly into the pan.

2 Fry at 375 degrees, or the same temperature as your fish, turning once to brown on each side. Serves 4. To multiply the recipe for large groups, figure one egg for each two additional cups of meal mix, and add enough liquid to provide a consistency thick enough to hold shape.

BATTER FRIED FISH

- ✔ 2 eggs
- ✔ ½ tsp. sugar
- ✔ 4 heaping tbsp. flour
- ✔ ½ tsp. salt
- ✔ ⅛ tsp. black pepper
- ✔ Milk to obtain consistency of heavy cream
- ✔ Salt and pepper

Deep-frying is the only suitable method for cooking batter-coated fish, which is the type used in fish and chips. Traditionally, the "chips" are cut from potatoes with the skin on, and served with a splash of vinegar. But ordinary French fries, whether frozen or home-made, are now the popular choice. You might also prefer to serve them on a paper plate instead of the tradition-al rolled-up newspaper.

1 Mix the flour, sugar, salt and pepper.

2 In a separate bowl, beat the eggs with the milk by hand, then add the dry mix a little at a time and continue beating until smooth.

3 Using a fork, dip the fish pieces into the batter. Allow excess batter to drip away, and then drop the pieces individually into 350-degree oil.

Remove with a slotted spoon or basket and drain the pieces on several layers of newspaper. Yes, you could also drain on paper towels or better yet, a mix of the two with the towels on top.

FISH FRIED IN CRUMBS OR INSTANT POTATO

This procedure is best done with three shallow bowls; one for the egg, the others for flour and crumbs.

1 Wet the pieces of fish and sprinkle them with salt and pepper, very lightly if seasoned crumbs are used.

2 Dip fish in beaten egg, then dredge in flour, then in beaten egg once more and, finally, in the crumbs or dry potato, coating thoroughly. *Hold fish on a plate or paper towels until cooking begins.*

If fillets are thin, around one-quarter inch, fry them at 350 degrees or so, turning once. They will brown very quickly, probably in a minute or so per side. Thicker pieces of fish, one-half to one inch thick, must be fried longer and at lower temperature, no more than 325 degrees. In either case, the fish will be done when the color is right: Rich golden or brown, but not too dark.

✓ **Fish fillets or boneless pieces of large fillets**

✓ **Salt and pepper**

✓ **Beaten egg**

✓ **Flour**

✓ **Prepared bread crumbs or cracker meal or cornflake crumbs or instant mashed potato**

With any of these coatings, deep-frying and pan-frying are equally suitable. Bread crumbs are sold plain or with various seasonings. If you prefer your own seasonings, such as seasoned salt, lemon-pepper or Cajun, choose among plain bread crumbs, cracker meal, instant mashed potato, or cornflake crumbs. The latter make a scrumptious coating, provided you use commercially packaged flakes. Crushing your own cornflakes doesn't produce the same result.

PAN-FRYING AND SAUTÉING

These methods differ from deep-frying in that they employ less oil. Sautéing (sometimes called pan-broiling) simply means cooking without any flour or other coating, whereas pan-frying indicates a coating of flour or other crust. Here, however, the terms are used interchangeably because, regardless of whether the fish is coated or not, cooking procedures remain essentially the same.

The choice between deep-frying and pan-frying is often merely a personal one, but efficiency should be considered too. If you have only a few pieces of fish to cook for one or two diners, why haul out a deep pan and lots of grease, when you can get the same results with far less oil in a small pan? Save deep-frying for times when there are more than a couple of hungry mouths to feed.

You can use either a traditional iron skillet or an aluminum pan with just a light coating of butter, margarine or oil. Perhaps the best treatment is to coat the pan lightly with canola or other vegetable oil, tossing in just a small pat of butter to add flavor and assist in browning. For the ultimate in healthy cooking (of uncoated fish), you can even employ a nonstick pan with no more than a squirt of olive oil or butter-flavored spray.

The best temperature setting is around 325-350 degrees, medium to medium-high. Any higher and the surface might brown much too fast, perhaps even scorching before the fish is cooked through. This is especially true when using butter or margarine.

Sautéed fish should be turned only once, as soon as the first side is browned. And here it should be pointed out that "browned" is a relative term. Without a coating, fish often do not really take on the rich brown hue provided by batter or crumbs, although the color can be deepened by cooking the fillets in browned butter or margarine. Anyway, the fish should be turned when the edges take on a crisp gold or brownish tone while most of the center portion is an appetizing yellowish-tan. After turning and cooking for another minute or two, test for doneness with a fork, piercing gently to make sure the meat flakes through (or flakes to the bone in the case of whole fish).

FISH PARMESAN

- ✔ ¼ pound per person of firm, white fish
- ✔ Salt and pepper
- ✔ Beaten egg
- ✔ Flour
- ✔ Italian flavored bread crumbs
- ✔ Olive oil
- ✔ Shredded or sliced mozzarella cheese
- ✔ Grated Parmesan cheese
- ✔ Italian red sauce of choice, already prepared (or canned)

1. Heat the red sauce in a separate pan and maintain at low setting.

2. Dip fish in beaten egg, then dredge in flour, then back in beaten egg, and finally in bread crumbs.

   Pan-fry in a small amount of olive oil at medium setting.

3. After turning, cover top of fish with mozzarella. By the time the mozzarella melts the other side of the fish should be brown.

   Remove to individual plates, spoon the red sauce over all and sprinkle liberally with grated Parmesan. Serve with pasta of your choice.

Not much different from traditional veal parmesan, this dish works best with fish of very dense flesh, such as shark, amberjack, pompano or grouper, which should be sliced quite thin, about one-quarter of an inch.

BLACKENED FISH

- ✔ **Fish fillets**
- ✔ **1 ½ tsp. cayenne pepper**
- ✔ **1 ½ tsp. paprika**
- ✔ **3 tsp. salt**
- ✔ **1 tsp. onion powder**
- ✔ **1 tsp. garlic powder**
- ✔ **½ tsp. white pepper**
- ✔ **½ tsp. black pepper**
- ✔ **½ tsp. oregano**
- ✔ **½ tsp. thyme**

Mix all ingredients thoroughly. Blackening works best with firm-fleshed fish such as redfish, amberjack, tuna and grouper, but can be used with any species you like.

1. Coat single-serving pieces with olive oil or melted butter and then dip or dust them liberally with the blackening mix.

2. Classic blackened fish requires a cast iron skillet, which is allowed to get nearly red-hot. At that point, a half-stick of butter is dropped into the pan, followed an instant later by the fillets, which are cooked no more than two minutes a side. Add a bit more butter after turning, if needed. This approach, obviously, will create so much smoke that it's almost imperative to do the cooking outside.

An alternate method will allow you to stay in the kitchen— just barely—while turning out a blackened product that few would be able to tell from the "real" thing. For this, you can use any kind of skillet. Cast iron is still preferred, but an aluminum pan with a non-stick finish will do fine. Turn your stove's exhaust fan on high, and then place your skillet on a burner also set on high. Add a quarter of a stick of butter or margarine and when the butter turns dark brown—nearly black—put in two to four pieces of oiled and dusted fish. Cook about two minutes on each side, maintaining high heat. If more fish remains to be cooked, add more butter and again allow it to turn dark brown before proceeding.

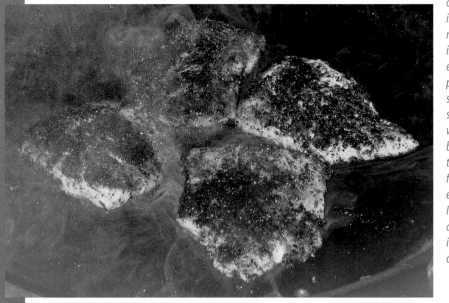

SAUTÉ AMANDINE

- ✓ **2 panfish or fish fillets**
- ✓ **Milk or buttermilk**
- ✓ **Flour for dredging**
- ✓ **Butter, margarine or oil for cooking**
- ✓ **Salt and pepper**
- ✓ **¼ cup sliced almonds (more if desired)**
- ✓ **Parsley, small amount, chopped**
- ✓ **Lemon juice**

Many kinds of fish are suitable for this recipe, including whole small trout or panfish, plus fillets of nearly any popular species from sea or lake. Soak fish in milk, in refrigerator, for at least an hour.

1 Sprinkle fish with salt and pepper and dredge in flour.

2 Cover bottom of frying pan with olive oil, melted butter, or melted margarine. Sauté the fish on medium to medium-high heat until brown, turning once. Remove fish from pan.

3 Drain away any excess oil. Add sliced almonds and a little more butter or oil, if needed.

4 Stir until almonds are light brown. Add chopped parsley and stir.

Pour over fish and sprinkle with lemon juice. Serves 2.

SPICY SAUTÉ AMANDINE

- ✔ **3-4 panfish or 2 pounds fillets**
- ✔ **1 egg**
- ✔ **1 cup milk**
- ✔ **Flour**
- ✔ **½ cup butter**
- ✔ **¼ cup almonds, sliced**
- ✔ **2 tbsp. Worcestershire sauce**
- ✔ **Juice of 2 lemons**
- ✔ **Salt and pepper**

1. Salt and pepper the fish.
2. Beat egg and milk together. Dip fish in egg-milk mixture and dredge in flour.
3. In skillet, melt butter and sauté fish at medium heat until brown on both sides.

Remove fish. Add almonds to skillet and brown. Add lemon juice and Worcestershire sauce. Pour over fish. Serves 3 or 4.

FISH AND EGG SCRAMBLE

1. Saute onion in butter over medium heat until transparent. Reduce heat to low. Add flaked fish.
2. Beat eggs, then beat in milk and Worcestershire sauce and pour mixture into skillet with onion.

Cook, stirring constantly, until eggs are as firm as you like them. Salt and pepper to taste. Serves 3 or 4.

- ✔ **1 cup cooked fish**
- ✔ **1 small onion, chopped**
- ✔ **2 tbsp. butter**
- ✔ **6 eggs**
- ✔ **¼ cup milk**
- ✔ **1 tsp. Worcestershire sauce**
- ✔ **Salt and pepper**

SAUTÉED SMOKED FISH WITH EGGS

If serving-size pieces of smoked fish are used, sauté them in butter at medium-low temperature just long enough to heat well, turning once.

Scramble the eggs in the same pan and serve over the fish. If small bits of smoked fish are used, simply mix them with the beaten eggs and scramble all together.

- ✔ **Smoked fish fillets or small pieces**
- ✔ **1 tbsp. butter**
- ✔ **Eggs, beaten with salt, pepper and a little milk**

SAUTÉED FISH IN SOUR CREAM

- ✔ **2 pounds fillets or steaks**
- ✔ **Flour**
- ✔ **Salt and pepper**
- ✔ **½ tsp. basil, crushed**
- ✔ **1 cup sour cream**
- ✔ **¼ cup butter or oil**
- ✔ **1 onion, sliced**

1. Cut fish into serving-size pieces. Sprinkle with salt and pepper. Dredge in flour.
2. Sauté onion in butter until tender.
3. Sauté fish at medium heat, turning once, until golden brown on both sides.

Cover fish with onion, basil and sour cream.

Cover and simmer gently for 3 minutes or until fish meets test for doneness. Serves 3 or 4.

SAUTÉED FISH WITH VEGETABLES

✓ **2 pounds fish fillets**

✓ **½ stick butter or margarine**

✓ **Seasoned salt**

✓ **¼ cup white wine**

✓ **1 medium onion, sliced**

✓ **3 vegetables (at least) from among the following:**

✓ **1 stalk celery, chopped**

✓ **1 small yellow squash, sliced**

✓ **1 small zucchini, sliced**

✓ **1 red or green pepper, sliced**

✓ **1 ripe but firm tomato cut in small wedges**

1 Sprinkle fillets with seasoned salt.

2 Melt butter or margarine in a large sauté pan at medium heat and continue heating until butter covers the bottom of the pan and turns dark brown.

3 Add fish fillets. Turn after about 30 seconds and brown other side for another half-minute. Remove fillets to a nearby platter.

Fish need not be done at this point, only browned on both sides.

4 Add onion and vegetables of your choice and cook, stirring frequently, until onion is opaque and other vegetables thoroughly heated. Do not overcook.

5 Sprinkle vegetables lightly with seasoned salt (or salt and black pepper). Add wine.

6 Place fish fillets atop vegetables, cover, reduce heat and simmer for about five minutes. Check fish for doneness.

All but the thickest fillets should be cooked. If not, simmer a few minutes more. Serves 4 or 5.

PAN-FRIED TROUT, RUSSIAN STYLE

- ✔ **6 to 8 small stream trout, dressed**
- ✔ **2 eggs, beaten**
- ✔ **½ cup milk**
- ✔ **1 ½ cups prepared bread crumbs**
- ✔ **olive or vegetable oil for frying**
- ✔ **1 stick butter, soft**
- ✔ **2 hard-boiled eggs, chopped**
- ✔ **2 tbsp. pimento, chopped**
- ✔ **Salt and pepper**

1. Salt and pepper the trout.
2. Mix beaten eggs and milk; dip trout in mixture, then roll in bread crumbs.
3. Sauté in skillet at medium heat, using just a light covering of oil.
4. Make a paste of the butter, hard-boiled eggs and pimento. Spread paste over hot fish and serve immediately. Serves 6 or 8.

FISH CAKES

✔ **3 large potatoes**
✔ **¼ stick butter**
✔ **Salt and pepper**
✔ **1 egg**
✔ **½ cup evaporated milk**
✔ **1 cup flaked fish**

Although probably most often made with salmon or trout, this treatment glamorizes any leftover fish.

1. Boil potatoes, drain, and mash thoroughly. Add butter, some salt and pepper, and blend by stirring.
2. Beat egg and milk together and add to potatoes. Beat until light and fluffy. Add the fish and beat again.
3. Drop from spoon and pan-fry in a little oil at medium-high until brown, turning once. After turning, press with spatula to achieve desired thickness. Serves 6.

FAST FISH CHOW MEIN

1. Heat oils in a wok or non-stick skillet at medium-high setting.
2. Brown diced fish quickly on all sides. Add onion and cook, stirring with wooden spoon, for 2 minutes. Add soy sauce and reduce heat to low. Add chop suey vegetables. Stir until contents of pan are thoroughly heated.

Serve over rice for chop suey, or with Chinese noodles for chow mein. Serves 2 to 3.

✔ **1 pound fish fillet, diced**
✔ **1 can Chop Suey vegetables, well drained**
✔ **2 tbsp. vegetable oil**
✔ **1 medium onion, coarsely chopped**
✔ **1 tsp. soy sauce**
✔ **Dash sesame oil**

Chow mein and chop suey are essentially the same dish, differing only in that chop suey is served over rice and chow mein over Chinese noodles. But both are often served together. Does this make the dish chop mein? Chow suey? Only a student of pseudo-Chinese would know for sure. The rest of us don't really care.

FISH in the OVEN
Baking, Whole and Stuffed Fish

A whole baked fish, either with or without the head, is one of the most attractive dishes you can put on the table—and it tastes even better than it looks. Some folks may not like the idea of a fish head staring up at them from the platter, but there is a practical side as well as a visual one. The head of a fish contains a surprising amount of tasty meat—mostly around the "cheeks" and the top of the head. For many diners, this makes a special treat.

At any rate, the prime baking size is from two to eight pounds. You can, of course, bake fish weighing a pound or less, but will have to allot at least one fish per person.

BAKING TIPS

This magnificent mutton snapper is a prime candidate for baking whole. It can be stuffed with crabmeat and cooked over an open fire. Don't forget the Cajun spice.

Your first step in baking is to select a non-stick baking pan or cover a shallow pan with aluminum foil. On this, place the dressed fish, which has been patted dry with a paper towel. The fish can be stuffed or not, as you like. Make sure the oven has been preheated to 350 degrees, and then put the pan on a shelf in the center of the oven.

Although the skin helps retain the juices, you should still do a little basting, either by brushing or by letting the fish heat for a few minutes, and then rubbing the surface with a pat of butter. After about 10 or 15 minutes, rub again with butter.

If your dietician isn't looking, you might use bacon as a self-baster. Before putting your fish in the oven, lay two or more strips of bacon across the top. No further basting will be needed, and the skin protects the fish from absorbing more than just a delicate hint of bacon flavor.

Cooking time will vary from as little as 20 minutes for a two-pound fish to an hour or more for an eight-pounder. Again, you should rely on testing more than timing, and avoid cooking too long. With a two- or three-pound fish, test with a fork after about 20 minutes. At the thickest portion, the meat should flake to the bone and not show any pink.

One reason testing is important is because thermostats on many ovens may not be accurate. Whether the fish is put in cold or at room temperature can make a difference, too. Fish weighing less than two pounds will normally bake to perfection in about 20 minutes. Otherwise, they should be treated exactly like larger ones—by basting with butter or bacon strips. When you bake fillets or steaks rather than whole fish, they should be basted very liberally or else wrapped in aluminum foil with a liberal coat of butter or margarine, to prevent drying.

Remember that simple baked fish—whether it be a whole, dressed fish, steaks or fillets—requires little more than salt and some butter or other fat for basting. But many attractive variations are available, and they can add not only changes in taste, but in texture and appearance as well.

FILLETS EN PAPILLOTE

1 Sprinkle fish with salt and pepper. Combine butter, lemon juice, dill and salt. Cut fillets into 6 equal portions.

2 Cut 6 squares of heavy aluminum foil, 12 inches square. Place 1 teaspoon of butter mixture on each of 3 foil squares and lay two portions of fish on top of each. Then add an onion slice, another teaspoon of the butter mixture and, finally, a slice of cheese.

Cover with the other pieces of foil and seal the edges of the packets. Bake at 400 degrees for about 15 minutes. Serves 6.

- ✔ **2 pounds fillets**
- ✔ **½ cup melted butter**
- ✔ **1 tbsp. lemon juice**
- ✔ **½ tsp. dill**
- ✔ **1 onion, sliced thin**
- ✔ **3 slices processed Swiss cheese**
- ✔ **Salt and pepper**

BAKED, STUFFED FISH

- ✔ 1 fish, 3 or 4 pounds, dressed for baking, or two large fillets
- ✔ Olive oil or melted butter
- ✔ Salt and pepper

1 Sprinkle fish liberally with salt and pepper, inside and out. Rub fish with olive oil or brush with melted butter.

2 Place in a foil-lined baking pan. Fill cavity of fish with selected stuffing—choosing from those that follow or a traditional family favorite.

Bake at 350 degrees for about 30 minutes, or until fork pierces easily to the bone at thickest part. Extra stuffing can be wrapped in foil and baked alongside. If fillets are used for this recipe, place them in a single layer in greased shallow baking dish.

Spoon stuffing on each fillet and press lightly. Bake at 350 degrees for 30 to 40 minutes or until fish flakes easily with a fork. Serves 6.

STUFFINGS
Each will stuff a three- to six-pound fish. Extra stuffing can be cooked in aluminum foil outside the fish.

QUICK CLAM STUFFING

✔ ¼ cup chopped onion
✔ ½ stick butter
✔ One 8-ounce package seasoned stuffing mix
✔ One 6½-ounce can minced clams

Sauté onion in butter until clear. Remove pan from burner and add stuffing mix and clams, including liquid from can.

Mix well. If stuffing is too dry for your taste, add just a little water.

CORNBREAD STUFFING

✔ 3 tbsp. melted butter
✔ 1 small onion, chopped
✔ 1 cup celery, chopped
✔ 1 tbsp. lemon juice
✔ ½ tsp. salt
✔ 2 cups soft bread crumbs
✔ 1 cup cornbread, crumbled

Sauté onion and celery in butter until soft.

Add other ingredients and toss well but lightly.

RICE-MUSHROOM STUFFING

✔ ½ cup butter
✔ 1 large onion, minced
✔ 2 cups celery, minced
✔ 1 cup sliced mushrooms
✔ 2½ cups cooked rice
✔ ½ tsp. each salt, pepper, sage, thyme

Melt butter, and sauté onion, celery and mushrooms about 3 minutes until soft, but not brown.

Add other ingredients and mix thoroughly.

BREAD STUFFING

✔ 6 tbsp. melted butter
✔ 1 small onion, chopped
✔ 1 cup celery, chopped
✔ 3 cups dry bread crumbs
✔ 1 tsp. each: salt, thyme, sage
✔ Dash of pepper

Sauté onions and celery in butter until soft, not brown.

Put crumbs and seasonings in a bowl and add the sautéed vegetables.

Toss thoroughly. If dressing seems too dry, add a couple of tablespoons of water to moisten.

SOUR CREAM STUFFING

✔ Melted butter
✔ 1 small onion, chopped
✔ 1 cup celery, chopped
✔ 4 cups dry bread cubes
✔ ½ cup sour cream
✔ 2 tbsp. grated lemon rind
✔ 1 tsp. paprika
✔ 1 tsp. salt

Cook celery and onion in butter until tender.

Combine all ingredients and mix thoroughly.

BAKED FILLETS HAWAIIAN

- ✔ Rice-mushroom stuffing
- ✔ 1 cup crushed pineapple, well drained
- ✔ 2 large fish fillets, skinned or skin-on
- ✔ 3 slices bacon (optional)

Mix pineapple with stuffing and spread between fillets. If skin is on the fillets, brush top generously with butter before baking at 350 degrees for about 20 minutes. Test for flakiness with fork.

If fillets have no skin, you may wish to place bacon slices across the top to eliminate need for basting. Serves 2 to 4, depending on fillet size.

BAKED FILLETS ALICANTE

- ✔ 1 onion, sliced
- ✔ 1 pound fillets or steaks about 1 inch thick
- ✔ ¼ cup olive oil or vegetable oil
- ✔ ½ cup brown gravy (from mix or left over)
- ✔ ½ cup white wine
- ✔ ¼ tsp. salt
- ✔ Sprinkling of pepper
- ✔ ¼ cup nuts, finely chopped

Spread onion slices in bottom of casserole or foil-lined baking dish. Place fish in dish.

Mix other ingredients well and pour over fish. Bake at 350 degrees for 15-20 minutes. Serves 2 or 3.

FILLETS IN SAVORY SAUCE

- ✔ **1 or 1½ pounds fish fillets**
- ✔ **1 tbsp. melted butter**
- ✔ **1 pkg. frozen asparagus or broccoli pieces**
- ✔ **2 tbsp. butter**
- ✔ **2 tbsp. flour**
- ✔ **1 cup milk**
- ✔ **1 cup bread crumbs**
- ✔ **½ cup American cheese**
- ✔ **½ cup processed Swiss cheese**
- ✔ **2 tbsp. melted butter**
- ✔ **Salt and pepper**

1 Cook the frozen vegetables according to directions on package. Drain.

2 Cut fish into serving-size pieces, place in a greased baking dish, brush with melted butter and sprinkle with salt and pepper.

Bake for 10 minutes at 400 degrees.

3 While fish is baking, melt 2 tbsp. butter in a saucepan. Stir in flour and add dashes of salt and pepper. Add milk all at once, stir and bring to boiling point. Remove from burner and stir in the processed cheeses.

4 After 10 minutes, remove fish from oven and arrange asparagus or broccoli pieces on top. Pour sauce over all.

5 Combine bread crumbs with 2 tbsp. melted butter and sprinkle over the fillets. Return to oven and bake a few minutes longer, until lightly browned. Serves 4.

BAKED FILLETS WITH CRAB AND SHRIMP

1. Sprinkle fish with salt and pepper.
2. Melt butter in pan and stir in flour. Slowly add milk. Stir until smooth and thickened. Remove from heat and stir in other ingredients.
3. Roll up filling inside the fillets, securing with toothpicks. Brush outside of fillets with melted butter.

Bake at 400 degrees for about 20-25 minutes, basting twice more. Serves 6 or 7.

- ✔ 3 pounds fillets
- ✔ 2 tbsp. butter
- ✔ 2 tbsp. flour
- ✔ 2 cups milk
- ✔ ¼ cup each crabmeat and cooked shrimp, chopped
- ✔ 1 small onion, chopped
- ✔ ¼ cup celery
- ✔ Salt and pepper

SANDY'S SEAFOOD SURPRISE

- ✔ 8 or 10 small fish fillets (crappie or other pan-fish)
- ✔ 1 pound bay scallops
- ✔ 1 medium onion, chopped
- ✔ 1 large tomato, ripe but firm, chopped
- ✔ ¼ cup celery, chopped
- ✔ 1 bell pepper, chopped
- ✔ ½ pound fresh mushrooms, sliced
- ✔ ¼ pound grated Swiss cheese
- ✔ ¼ pound grated mild cheddar cheese
- ✔ Olive oil
- ✔ Seasoned salt

1 Rub fillets with olive oil. Spread fillets, intermingled with scallops, to cover the bottom of a non-stick shallow baking pan.

Deep-sea scallops may be substituted for bay scallops, but should be quartered or cut to approximate thickness of fish.

2 Sprinkle fish and scallops very lightly with seasoned salt. Lightly toss together all chopped vegetables and spread evenly over the seafood. Mix grated cheeses together and sprinkle over all.

Bake at 450 degrees for 10 minutes Serves 6.

This recipe is easily "customized" to your taste. For instance, you can use all fish or all scallops, or add other seafood. And the mix of vegetables can include sliced or chopped carrots, cauliflower, broccoli, etc. Use your own favorites (or what you have on hand).

BAKED FILLETS IN WINE

1. Place fillets in foil-lined pan and sprinkle with salt and pepper, or with seasoned salt.

2. Spread tomatoes over fillets, slicing tomatoes if whole. Pour wine over fish and sprinkle with basil.

Bake at 350 degrees for 10 minutes.

Remove and sprinkle with cheese. Bake about five minutes longer, or until fish flakes easily with fork. On serving, spoon juices over portions. Serves 3.

✔ **1 pound lean fish fillets**
✔ **1 cup canned tomatoes, well drained**
✔ **¼ cup white wine**
✔ **½ tsp. basil**
✔ **½ cup shredded Swiss cheese**
✔ **Salt and pepper**

OVEN-FRIED FISH

- 4-6 panfish or 1 to 2 pounds of steaks or fillets
- 1 egg, beaten
- Prepared bread crumbs or cornflake crumbs
- ½ cup butter, melted
- 1 lemon
- Salt and pepper

1. Salt and pepper the fish to taste, then dip in beaten egg and shake in a bag with the bread crumbs until well coated.

2. Place fish in a foil-lined baking pan (turn edges of foil up to form an inner dish). Squeeze lemon into butter and drizzle over coated fish.

Bake at 500 degrees for 8 or 10 minutes, until crust is golden and fish tests done with a fork. Serves 4 to 6.

FISH FILLETS 'N RICE

This recipe is best when used with four fillets, about six inches long each.

1 Sprinkle fish with salt and pepper. Combine eggs, parsley, mayonnaise and mustard.

2 Spoon one fourth of the mixture atop each of two fillets. Combine broccoli and rice.

3 In separate bowl, stir together soup and wine until smooth. Stir one cup of the soup-wine mix into rice mixture.

4 Put rice mixture into baking dish and spread evenly. Put fish atop rice. Pour remaining soup-wine mix over fish.

Cover with foil and bake at 375 degrees for 10 minutes. Remove foil and bake 5-10 minutes more, until fish flakes with fork. Serves 4.

✔ 1 pound or so fish fillets
✔ 3 hard-boiled eggs, chopped
✔ 2 tbsp. parsley, chopped
✔ 2 tbsp. mayonnaise
✔ ½ tsp. mustard
✔ 1 pkg. frozen chopped broccoli, well thawed
✔ 2 cups cooked rice
✔ 1 can cream of shrimp soup
✔ ½ cup white wine
✔ Salt and pepper

FISH 'N SWISS

- ✔ **1 pound fillets**
- ✔ **2 tbsp. chopped parsley**
- ✔ **½ cup shredded Swiss cheese**
- ✔ **1 tbsp. butter**
- ✔ **1 tbsp. flour**
- ✔ **¼ tsp. salt**
- ✔ **Pepper**
- ✔ **½ cup evaporated milk**
- ✔ **2 tbsp. sherry**

Use four fillets about six inches long apiece.

1. Sprinkle fillets with parsley and salt lightly. Place one fourth of cheese on each fillet and roll up.

2. In a saucepan, melt butter and stir in flour. Sprinkle lightly with salt and pepper and stir again. Add milk and sherry all at once. Stir and cook until mixture is thickened and bubbling.

3. Place fish rolls in a shallow baking dish and pour sauce over.

Bake uncovered at 400 degrees for 15-20 minutes or until fish flakes easily with a fork.

If desired, additional cheese can be sprinkled on top and melted by placing in oven for 2 or 3 more minutes.
Serves 4.

FAST FILLETS FLORENTINE

1 Cook spinach according to directions. Drain. Spread spinach in a pie plate.

2 Use four fish fillets about six inches long. Season each with salt and pepper and spread one-eighth of the cream cheese on each. Roll up the fillets and place on top of the spinach.

3 In large skillet or saucepan, melt the butter and stir in the flour. Sprinkle lightly with salt and pepper. Add six ounces of water and the bouillon cube. Heat, stirring gently, until thick and bubbling. Remove from heat. Gradually stir in remaining cream cheese. Stir in wine.

Pour over fillets and sprinkle with paprika. Bake at 350 degrees for 15-20 minutes. Serves 4.

✔ **1 pound fillets**
✔ **1 pkg. frozen whole-leaf spinach**
✔ **1 pkg. (4 oz.) whipped cream cheese**
✔ **1 tbsp. butter**
✔ **4 tbsp. flour**
✔ **1 cube chicken bouillon**
✔ **1 tbsp. white wine**
✔ **Salt, pepper, paprika**

CRABBY FILLETS

- ✔ **2 pounds fish fillets**
- ✔ **1 can chopped mush-rooms**
- ✔ **1 cup milk**
- ✔ **¼ onion, chopped**
- ✔ **¼ cup butter**
- ✔ **1 can crabmeat**
- ✔ **½ cup coarsely crushed saltines**
- ✔ **2 tbsp. minced parsley**
- ✔ **½ tsp. salt**
- ✔ **Pepper**
- ✔ **3 tbsp. butter**
- ✔ **3 tbsp. flour**
- ✔ **¼ cup white wine**
- ✔ **1 cup shredded Swiss cheese**
- ✔ **½ tsp. paprika**

Use eight fillets about six inches long each.

1 Drain mushrooms, reserving liquid. Add milk to liquid and set aside.

2 In skillet, sauté onion in ¼ cup butter until soft. Add mushrooms, crabmeat, crumbs, parsley, ¼ tsp. salt and a dash of pepper, and spread over fillets.

3 Fold each fillet over the filling, sticking narrow end underneath. Place fillets, tucked side down, in a baking dish.

4 In saucepan, melt butter. Stir in flour and ¼ tsp. salt. Add the milk, liquid from mushrooms and wine. Heat, stirring, until thick and bubbling. Pour over fillets.

Bake at 400 degrees for 20 minutes. Sprinkle with cheese and paprika and return to oven for 5 minutes longer to brown. Serves 8.

BAKED FI...

1. Sprinkle fish inside and out with salt and pepper and place in a baking dish or casserole. Pour tomatoes and tomato sauce over fish.

2. Scatter diced peppers and sliced onion over all.

   Cover (aluminum foil is fine) and bake at 425 degrees for 30 minutes to an hour, depending on thickness of fish used. Test after 30 minutes with a fork. Serves 4 to 6.

- ✓ One 4-...
  three sm...
  baking
- ✓ One 1-pound ca...
- ✓ ½ cup tomato sauc...
- ✓ 1 small can jalapeno peppers, diced
- ✓ 1 onion, sliced thin
- ✓ Salt and pepper

...ED FISH WITH REALLY WILD STUFFING

- ✔ One 3- to 4-pound fish, dressed for baking
- ✔ 4 oz. wild rice
- ✔ 1 cup sliced fresh mushrooms
- ✔ ¼ cup butter
- ✔ 1 cup frozen peas, thawed
- ✔ ¼ cup chopped onion
- ✔ 2 tbsp. chopped pimento
- ✔ 2 tbsp. lemon juice
- ✔ 2 tbsp. melted butter

Cook wild rice according to instructions on package.

1. Sauté mushrooms in butter until tender. Combine rice, mushrooms, peas, onion, pimento and lemon juice.
2. Sprinkle fish with salt. Fill with stuffing and skewer cavity. Brush fish with melted butter.

Bake at 350 degrees for 45 minutes to one hour or until fork pierces easily to bone at thickest part.

Wrap any extra stuffing in foil and bake with fish for last 20 minutes. Brush fish once or twice more with butter during cooking. Serves 6.

BAKED FISH WITH NEARLY WILD STUFFING

1 In large saucepan, sauté mushrooms, carrots, onion and parsley in butter until tender. Add rice and the seasoning mix from rice package. Stir well. Add water and heat to boiling. Add bouillon and a sprinkle of pepper and stir until cube dissolves. Cover and cook over low heat for 20 minutes.

2 Place fish in a greased baking pan. Brush inside and out with 3 tbsp. of melted butter. Sprinkle inside and out with salt and pepper. Stuff with rice mixture.

Wrap extra stuffing in heavy foil and place near fish for about last 30 minutes of baking time.

Bake fish at 350 degrees for about an hour, or until fork pierces easily to bone at thickest part. Serves 8.

- ✔ One 4- to 6-pound fish, dressed for baking
- ✔ 1½ cups sliced fresh mushrooms
- ✔ 1 cup shredded carrot
- ✔ ¼ cup chopped onion
- ✔ ¼ cup chopped parsley
- ✔ ¼ cup butter
- ✔ ¼ tsp. salt
- ✔ One 6-oz. pkg. wild rice/brown rice mix
- ✔ 2½ cups water
- ✔ 1 chicken bouillon cube
- ✔ 3 tbsp. melted butter

ZESTY BAKED FISH

- ✔ 1 or 2 fish, 3-4 pounds total, prepared for baking
- ✔ 2 cups Italian seasoned bread crumbs
- ✔ 1 onion, chopped fine
- ✔ ¼ cup sour cream
- ✔ 1 large dill pickle, chopped fine
- ✔ ½ tsp. paprika
- ✔ Olive oil
- ✔ Salt and pepper

1 Sprinkle fish with salt and pepper and place in an oiled baking dish.

2 Combine crumbs, onion, sour cream, pickle and paprika in a bowl.

Place stuffing in cavity of fish (or fishes), brush fish with olive oil, cover the pan (foil is fine) and bake at 425 degrees for 30 to 45 minutes.

1. Cut fillets into serving-size pieces. Sprinkle with salt and pepper and place on foil-lined pan or cookie sheet.

2. Drizzle oil over fish and arrange tomato slices on top. Sprinkle basil liberally over all.

Bake quickly in 500-degree oven for 10 to 12 minutes. Test with fork. Garnish individual servings with olives. Serves 3 or 4.

✔ 2

✔ Sl

✔ 1

✔ 2

✔ Sliced ripe, green, or black olives

✔ Salt and pepper

FISH EXOTICA

- whole fish, dressed, about 6 pounds
- ✔ ¼ cup lime juice
- ✔ 3 cups salted cashew nuts, chopped
- ✔ ¼ pound cheddar cheese, grated
- ✔ 1 small onion, grated
- ✔ 2 bay leaves, crushed
- ✔ 1 cup dry bread crumbs
- ✔ 1 cup milk
- ✔ ½ stick melted butter
- ✔ ¼ cup sherry

1 Rub fish inside and out with lime juice and sprinkle with salt. Place in foil-lined baking pan.

2 Mix 2½ cups of chopped nuts with the grated cheese, onion, and half the bread crumbs. Pour in milk and stir to make a thick paste.

Cover fish with paste and sprinkle on the remaining bread crumbs. Bake at 375 degrees for about 45 minutes.

In testing for doneness, ease fish up with spatula and test from bottom. Do not break the crust.

About three times while fish is baking, dribble mixture of butter and sherry over the top. When done, remove to platter and sprinkle with remaining nuts. Serves 4 to 6.

BAKED FISH, SPANISH STYLE

1 Sauté onion in olive oil. Add tomatoes and simmer for 5 minutes. Add other ingredients, except fish, and blend.

Place fish in foil-lined baking dish. Pour sauce over and bake in 350-degree oven for 30 to 40 minutes.

If using whole fish, allow longer cooking time and spoon sauce over fish several times while baking. Serves 4 to 6.

- ✔ 1 whole dressed fish, about 6 pounds or 3 to 4 pounds of fillets
- ✔ 1 large onion, chopped
- ✔ ¼ cup olive oil
- ✔ 1 No. 2½ can tomatoes
- ✔ 1 tbsp. capers
- ✔ 3-oz. jar stuffed olive bits
- ✔ 1 tsp. salt
- ✔ ½ tsp. black pepper
- ✔ 2 tsp. chili powder (optional)

FILLETS WITH SOUR CREAM AND MAYONNAISE

- ✔ **2 pounds fillets**
- ✔ **1½ cups sour cream**
- ✔ **½ cup mayonnaise**
- ✔ **2 scallions, chopped**
- ✔ **½ tsp. salt**
- ✔ **½ tsp. pepper**
- ✔ **4 tsp. lime juice**

1 Place fillets on foil-lined baking dish. Mix other ingredients together and spread over fish.

Bake at 375 degrees for 20-30 minutes. Serves 3 or 4.

BAKED FISH, FAST BUT FANCY

✔ **2 pounds fillets or steaks**
✔ **Salt and pepper**
✔ **1 can condensed soup**

1 Place fillets in foil-lined baking pan and sprinkle with salt and pepper.

2 Pour soup (any kind, according to your taste or mood—tomato, mushroom, celery, shrimp, cheddar cheese) into bowl and stir it well. Add a bit of milk to thin it a little if desired, but don't mix in another whole can of liquid as the directions on the can prescribe.

Pour soup over fish. Bake in a 400-degree oven about 20 minutes or until tender. If soup doesn't cover fish entirely, baste frequently during cooking. Serve over rice. Serves 3 or 4.

FISH STEAKS WITH A LATIN FLAIR

- ✔ **4 to 6 fish steaks**
- ✔ **2 tomatoes, sliced**
- ✔ **¼ cup thin-sliced cucumber**
- ✔ **¼ cup chopped onion**
- ✔ **¼ chopped green pepper**
- ✔ **1 clove garlic, crushed**
- ✔ **¼ stick butter**
- ✔ **2 tbsp. lemon juice**
- ✔ **Salt and pepper**

1 Place steaks in well-greased or foil-lined baking pan. Arrange slices of tomato and cucumber over steaks.

2 In skillet, sauté onion, pepper and garlic in butter until onion is clear. Stir in lemon juice. Sprinkle salt and pepper over fish and pour sauce over.

Bake at 375 degrees about 20 minutes, or until fish flakes easily with fork. Serves 6.

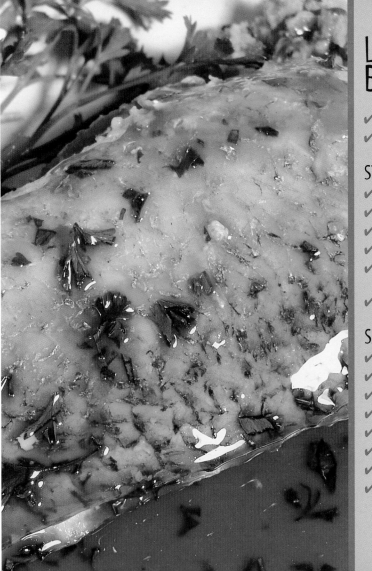

1. Cook celery, green pepper and chopped onion in 3 tbsp. butter until tender. Add stuffing mix and 3 tbsp. water. Stir well.

2. Place fish on sheet of greased heavy foil in shallow baking pan or sheet. Sprinkle salt and pepper on fish and in cavity. Fill cavity with stuffing mixture. Seal foil around fish.

Bake at 350 degrees for 20 minutes, then open foil and bake for about 10-15 minutes more, or until fork pierces easily to bone at thickest part.

3. While fish is baking, combine brown sugar and cornstarch in a saucepan. Stir in 2 tbsp. each of water, lemon juice and soy sauce. Add green onion, 1 tbsp. butter and garlic.

Cook until thick and bubbly, stirring constantly. Place fish on serving platter and pour sauce over. Serves 2 or 3.

LUAU BAKED FISH

- ✔ 2-pound fish, dressed for baking
- ✔ Salt and pepper

STUFFING

- ✔ ½ cup sliced celery
- ✔ ¼ cup chopped green pepper
- ✔ ¼ cup chopped onion
- ✔ 3 tbsp. butter
- ✔ 1½ cups packaged stuffing mix, herb seasoned
- ✔ 3 tbsp. water

SAUCE

- ✔ 1 tbsp. brown sugar
- ✔ 1 tsp. cornstarch
- ✔ 2 tbsp. water
- ✔ 2 tbsp. lemon juice
- ✔ 2 tbsp. soy sauce
- ✔ 2 tbsp. sliced green onion
- ✔ 1 tbsp. butter
- ✔ 1 clove garlic, minced

MORE FISH in the OVEN Broiling

Like baked fish, broiled fish is cooked in the oven but it receives direct, high heat from the broiler unit, rather than being surrounded by heat that is controlled at a specific temperature. To turn out delicious broiled fish, you must stay close to the scene of action in order to turn and baste the fish, when needed, and to guard against overcooking.

Broiled fish isn't so very different in taste from fish that's been cooked on the outside grill, but because it has no grill marks it isn't apt to be quite so appealing to the eye. There are, however, several ways in which you can increase its attractiveness. One way is simply to coat the "up" side with butter. Even though you use lighter oils for basting, a modest dollop of butter applied shortly before the finish will add a tempting brown tone to your broiled fish without adding many calories.

A liberal sprinkling of paprika adds appetizing color to broiled fish, just as it does to baked or steamed fish. And, finally, you can really add both eye appeal and taste appeal to broiled fish by topping it with a bit of shredded cheese and returning it to the broiler just long enough for the cheese to melt.

BROILING TIPS

Fish steaks an inch or more thick require turning. They should be brushed with butter or olive oil, to prevent drying out, and checked until flakey.

Steaks or fillets no more than a half-inch or so thick generally do not need turning. If thicker than that, they will probably need to be cooked a bit on both sides, but turning is no great problem.

Place the rack about four or five inches (no more) under the oven's broiler unit and allow a few minutes for pre-heating. Leave the door of the oven ajar.

Cover a cookie sheet or shallow broiling pan with aluminum foil, turning up the edges all around to avoid spillage and minimize cleanup.

Arrange your fish on the foil, skin side down if there is skin. Sprinkle with salt and black pepper, along with any other spices you elect to use. Place the pan under the broiler and keep it there just long enough to make the surface of the fish hot. Remove the pan and coat all fish generously with butter or margarine. Because the fish is hot, you can spear a pat of butter with a fork and slide this over each piece.

Now return the pan to the oven. Allow the fish to broil for about 5 or 6 minutes, then remove and check for doneness by sticking a fork gently into the thickest portion. The meat should flake easily all the way through. If it doesn't, apply another coating of butter and return to the oven for another few minutes.

If broiling a fish steak more than an inch thick, turn at the end of 5 or 6 minutes, brush with butter, and cook several more minutes. Again, testing with a fork is the only sure way to determine doneness, so don't wander away. Broiling is a pretty quick process.

Fatty fish, such as salmon, mackerel and bluefish need be treated no differently; however, they will need less basting.

Incidentally, all the broiling recipes given here are also adaptable to cooking on your outside grill (see Chapter 5).

BROILED STEAKS AU GRATIN

Place steaks in foil-lined baking pan. Brush with melted butter. Sprinkle on bread crumbs and grated cheese until each steak is covered.

Broil about 10 minutes. Salt and pepper to taste. Serves 4.

✔ **4 fish steaks, about ½ inch thick**
✔ **Butter**
✔ **1 cup bread crumbs**
✔ **½ cup cheddar cheese, grated (other kinds may be used)**
✔ **Salt and pepper**

SPICY BROILED FISH

- ✔ **2 pounds fillets**
- ✔ **½ cup steak sauce**
- ✔ **¼ cup ketchup**
- ✔ **¼ cup vegetable oil**
- ✔ **1 tbsp. vinegar**
- ✔ **1 tsp. salt**
- ✔ **½ tsp. curry powder**

Place fish skin-side up on foil-lined broiler pan, and spread with sauce made of other six ingredients.

Broil about 3 inches from broiler unit for 5 minutes. Turn fish carefully and spread other side with sauce. Broil until fish flakes when tested with fork. Serves 4.

BROILED STEAKS BERNAISE

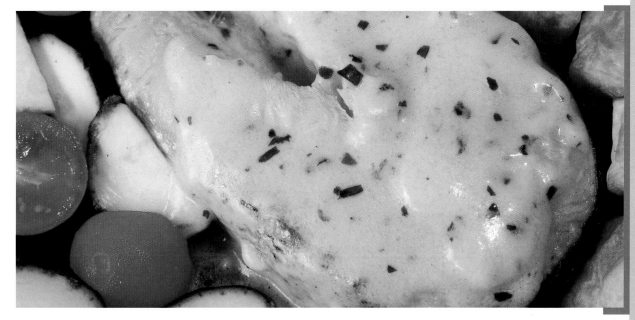

✔ **4 fish steaks, about ¼ to ½ pound each**

✔ **Salt and pepper**

✔ **Lemon juice**

Bernaise sauce

✔ **2 shallots or green onions, minced**

✔ **½ cup white wine**

✔ **½ cup white vinegar**

✔ **3 egg yolks**

✔ **¼ cup water**

✔ **1 cup clarified butter**

✔ **½ tsp. black pepper**

✔ **1 tsp. dried tarragon**

✔ **Lemon juice**

1 Preheat broiler and line a broiler pan with heavy aluminum foil.

2 Salt and pepper the steaks to taste and sprinkle with lemon juice. Set aside.

3 To make the sauce, heat wine and vinegar to boiling in a saucepan. Add shallots and simmer until only one tablespoon remains. Place this with egg yolks, pepper and water in top of a double boiler over simmering water. With a whisk, stir in the butter very gradually. Stir in lemon juice and tarragon. Turn off heat but keep the sauce in the double boiler to stay warm.

Broil steaks for about 8 minutes on one side and 3 or 4 minutes on the other. Test with fork. When fork pierces easily all the way through, the steaks are done. Pour sauce over individual servings.

OVEN BARBECUED STEAKS

- ✔ **4 fish steaks**
- ✔ **1 cup ketchup**
- ✔ **2 tbsp. olive oil**
- ✔ **½ tsp. minced garlic**
- ✔ **¼ tsp. black pepper**
- ✔ **8 drops Tabasco sauce**
- ✔ **1 tbsp. Worcestershire sauce**
- ✔ **2 tbsp. minced parsley**

1 In a bowl, mix all ingredients well.

While sauce is standing, preheat broiler and line a broiling pan with heavy aluminum foil.

2 Place steaks on foil and spread sauce over.

Broil for 6 minutes or so on one side, then turn, spread sauce over other side and broil for 3 or 4 more minutes, or until fork pierces through without resistance.

FRUITY FISH FILLETS

- ✔ 2 pounds fish fillets
- ✔ 1 small onion, grated
- ✔ 2 tbsp. lemon juice
- ✔ 2 tbsp. orange juice
- ✔ 2 tsp. grated orange rind
- ✔ ½ tsp. salt
- ✔ ⅛ tsp. grated nutmeg
- ✔ Black pepper

1. Arrange fillets in a greased shallow baking dish. Sprinkle with nutmeg and black pepper.
2. Combine other ingredients and pour over fish. Let stand for 15 or 20 minutes.

Place under broiler for 15 minutes—possibly longer if fillets are very thick. Baste once or twice during cooking. Serves 6.

ZIPPY BROILED FISH

- ✔ **2 pounds fish fillets**
- ✔ **1 clove garlic, minced**
- ✔ **5 sprigs dill or parsley, chopped**
- ✔ **½ stick butter**
- ✔ **½ tsp. salt**
- ✔ **½ tsp. coarse black pepper**

1 In a small saucepan, melt two tablespoons of butter with the parsley, salt, pepper and minced garlic. Mix well and remove from heat.

2 Brush fish well on both sides with plain butter and broil for 10 minutes in a shallow, foil-lined broiling pan.

3 Turn carefully, spread with more butter and broil five minutes longer. Pour butter-seasoning mixture over and broil another 5 minutes. Serves 5 or 6.

BROILED FISH STEAKS AU VIN

1. Place steaks in foil-lined pan and sprinkle with salt and pepper.
2. Place under broiler for a couple of minutes until surface of fish is hot.
3. Remove and brush each piece with a pat of butter held on a fork. Return to broiler and cook 5 or 6 minutes.
4. Remove again, spread more butter and splash liberally with white wine. Return to finish cooking, about 5 or 6 minutes. Sprinkle on a little more wine before serving.

✔ **Fish steaks, about one inch thick**
✔ **Salt and pepper**
✔ **Butter**
✔ **White wine**

QUICK AND SPICY BROILED FILLETS

✔ **2 pounds fillets**

✔ **Salt and pepper**

✔ **Lime juice**

✔ **½ cup French dressing**

NOTE: Either for convenience or added flavor from marinating, this dish can be prepared as instructed and placed in your refrigerator for anywhere from an hour to several hours before cooking. Broiling time will increase slightly.

1 Place fillets in foil-lined baking dish. Sprinkle with salt, pepper and lime juice.

2 Pour on the French dressing. Broil until done—about 5 or 10 minutes, according to thickness. Serves 3 or 4.

DEVILED BROILED FILLETS

✔ **2 pounds fillets**
✔ **½ cup chili sauce**
✔ **2 tbsp. mustard**
✔ **1 tbsp. Worcestershire sauce**
✔ **½ tsp. salt**
✔ **¼ tsp. pepper**

Place fillets in foil-lined pan. Mix all other ingredients and spread over fish. Broil for about 5 minutes until done. Serves 3 or 4.

BROILED FISH STEAKS ORIENTAL

- ✔ **2 pounds fish steaks**
- ✔ **¼ cup orange juice**
- ✔ **¼ cup soy sauce**
- ✔ **2 tbsp. ketchup**
- ✔ **2 tbsp. oil**
- ✔ **1 tbsp. lemon juice**
- ✔ **½ tsp. oregano**
- ✔ **½ tsp. pepper**
- ✔ **1 clove garlic, finely chopped**

1 Place fish in foil-lined baking dish. Combine all other ingredients and pour over fish; let stand for 30 minutes, turning once.

2 Remove and reserve sauce for basting. Place fish under broiler and broil about 4 to 5 minutes on each side, basting liberally with sauce at least twice on each side. Serves 3 or 4.

APPLE-CURRY FISH BROCHETTE

Tuna or shark is ideal for this recipe.

1 Cut fish into one-inch cubes. Sprinkle cubes with salt and pepper. Place in oiled, shallow baking dish.

2 Combine and mix all other ingredients. Pour over fish and let stand for 30 minutes, stirring occasionally.

Remove fish and place on skewers. Place skewers on a foil-covered cookie sheet and broil 3 to 4 minutes. Turn carefully, brush with remaining mixture and broil 3 minutes longer. Serve on rice. Serves 5 or 6.

✔ **1½ pounds thick fish fillets or steaks**
✔ **¼ cup oil**
✔ **¼ cup apple juice**
✔ **2 tbsp. chopped parsley**
✔ **1 tsp. curry powder**
✔ **Salt and pepper**

FISH in the OUTDOORS

Grilling, Smoke-Cooking, Smoking

D oes fish really taste better when you cook it outdoors? Of course it does, but not because any new or different flavors are gained from the fish itself. Taste, after all (and this is a scientific fact) is far more than the simple result of brushing food against taste buds. Many other elements contribute to the experience—aroma, texture, color, setting and good company among them. Considering the universal enthusiasm for out-of-doors cookery, it's strange indeed that people so seldom give thought to preparing fish on the home grill. Perhaps it's because they finally have mastered the perfect steak or hamburger, and are unwilling to risk their neighborhood reputations by trying something new. It could be, though, that they've tried to grill fish in the past, only to end up with a tough and tasteless product. Or maybe their fillets had flaked away and disappeared through the grill, burning on hot coals.

C H A P T E R F O U R

FISH-GRILLING TIPS

There's no doubt that grilling fish can be tricky for those whose barbecuing experience has been limited to red meat. Still, it certainly isn't difficult. The main thing to remember is that marinating and careful basting is the primary "secret" to scrumptious grilled fish.

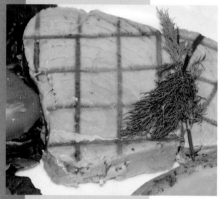

This prime tuna steak was lightly basted and then grilled over a low fire. Squeeze lemon juice over this and try a bite, and see if it isn't better than any sirloin steak.

Some types and cuts of fish handle much better than others when laid directly on the grill. Fish steaks, for example, are held together by their circling strip of skin. Whole fish, and fillets that have been scaled rather than skinned, will obviously be more cooperative than a skinless fillet, which is prone to crumbling and slipping through the grill.

Special screens that lie atop your grate represent one way of handling the chore with delicate types of fish, but the easiest solution is to use a hinged grilling basket that sandwiches the fish firmly between two wiremesh halves. You can baste right through the mesh, and there is an added advantage in that all your pieces of fish get turned over in one quick motion.

All fish should be marinated before grilling, not only to provide whatever flavor enhancements are favored by the cook, but also to help prevent sticking, since the popular marinades are oil-based. If you prefer not to allot the necessary marinating time, at least oil the fish liberally and coat it well with your favorite dry flavoring agents, such as lemon pepper, garlic pepper, or any of several commercial products

Generally, you will turn and baste any fish at least once during cooking, using melted butter with lemon juice, or remaining marinade. Average-size fillets and small whole fish will require two to five minutes of cooking on each side at medium-high heat. Larger fish take more time, of course. As always, the chef must be observant of cooking temperature and ever ready to adjust the thermometer (if provided on his covered gas or electric grill), or to raise or lower the grate (if cooking over coals). Until you're thoroughly familiar with your own grill's "personality," don't be embarrassed to keep consulting the instruction book.

You should aim for an attractive browned finish on the outside, with the inside moist and flaky. After a couple of tries, you'll probably be able to let your eyes be

your guide, but until you have built such confidence, fork-test the fish often for doneness. If you want a second check, use the fork to flake away meat down to the centermost portion. It's ready when the meat turns completely from opaque to white.

Another fine way to cook fish on your backyard grill (although to purists it doesn't really qualify for the name "grilled") is to wrap and seal heavy-duty aluminum foil around either a large fish or individual servings. Include butter or oil in the package, along with onion and whatever spices or other vegetables you choose. Place the package on the grill and turn it frequently with tongs. Check for doneness by removing the package and opening the foil—carefully, because of the steam. Cooking time will range from about 20 to 30 minutes for a whole small fish or thick steak, down to perhaps 10 or 15 minutes for small fillets. Take care that any potatoes and vegetables included in the individual packs are sliced thin enough to cook in the same amount of time.

Sure, you could turn out exactly the same dish in your kitchen oven or even in the coals of a campfire, but your guests will still be delighted. Aluminum-foil cookery is always much the same, whatever the food or the heat source.

As a matter of fact, any fish that can be broiled can also be prepared on an open grill, and any recipe for baked fish can be handled well on a covered grill.

To keep steaks from crumbling and slipping through the grill, use a grilling basket, above, or small-mesh screen, left.

MARINADES

The basic ingredient of most marinades is oil, wine or vinegar—or various combinations of those, along with spices or flavorings of choice. Following are a few combinations that are popular with fish, but feel free to amend any of them in any way you like, or to use a pet formula of your own. Regardless of what you choose, mix the ingredients thoroughly and place them in a covered bowl or a plastic bag that has a good sealing device, such as a twist-tie or zipper. Shake or stir to coat the pieces well, then marinate the fish for about an hour. Or all night, if using a whole, fairly large fish.

VINAIGRETTE MARINADE

- ✔ **1 small clove of garlic, crushed**
- ✔ **¼ tsp. salt**
- ✔ **½ tsp. spicy mustard**
- ✔ **2 tsp. lemon juice**
- ✔ **¼ cup olive oil**
- ✔ **1 tsp. red wine vinegar**
- ✔ **¼ tsp. fresh ground pepper**

HONEY-CITRUS MARINADE

- ✔ **½ tsp. orange zest**
- ✔ **¼ tsp. lemon zest**
- ✔ **¼ cup orange juice**
- ✔ **4 tsp. honey**
- ✔ **4 tsp. wine vinegar**

WINE-TARRAGON MARINADE

- ✔ **¼ cup dry sherry**
- ✔ **½ tsp. dried tarragon, finely chopped**
- ✔ **¼ tsp. garlic powder**
- ✔ **2 pinches ground ginger**
- ✔ **¼ cup olive oil**

SHERRY MARINADE

- ✔ **½ cup sherry wine**
- ✔ **1 tsp. garlic powder**
- ✔ **1 tsp. finely ground rosemary**

BASIL-BALSAMIC MARINADE

- ✔ **¾ cup olive oil**
- ✔ **½ cup tomato sauce**
- ✔ **¼ cup balsamic vinegar**
- ✔ **4 cloves crushed garlic**
- ✔ **¼ cup chopped fresh basil**
- ✔ **1 tsp. salt**
- ✔ **1 tsp. ground red pepper**

Marinades can be home-made, or store-bought. A large variety is available in some stores. Each imparts a different flavor and is guaranteed to spice up any seafood item.

SMOKE-COOKING

If you own a covered grill or one of the popular domed barbecue units often called a "kettle cooker" you can produce fish dishes that will make you the rave of the neighborhood. By means of a system called smoke-cooking or hot smoking, your fish will emerge with a marvelous smoky taste, and with much less time and effort than is required for true smoked fish.

The smoke is provided by hickory sawdust or chips soaked in a brine solution, made by dissolving half a cup of salt in three quarts of cold water. The chips should be soaked for about a half-hour in a quart of the solution. Other kinds of wood may be used, of course, to vary the flavor or to suit your own preference.

Your fish should be marinated too, for about 45 minutes, using either the same solution as for the chips or any marinade of your choice.

A low temperature is not required for smoke-cooking as it is with true smoking, because you are not really smoking the fish, just giving it a smoky flavor while it cooks. A good range is 250-300 degrees. With electric or gas grills you have only to set the thermostat. With a charcoal grill, use fewer briquettes than you would for ordinary grilling, and spread them out more thinly in the pan.

With a gas cooker, your soaked sawdust or chips can be placed on the cooking surface

handful of the chips or sawdust, making sure not to miss a coal.

When the grill is ready, remove your pieces of fish from the brine, rinse thoroughly and pat dry with a paper towel. Brush with vegetable oil, margarine or butter.

Place the fish directly on the grill or use the wireframe cage mentioned previously. Close the cover. The wet sawdust provides plenty of smoke. Raise the cover every ten to fifteen minutes to baste the fish liberally and to check the sawdust supply.

Add more wet wood as needed. And don't skimp on it. Cooking time may vary from as little as 30 minutes to, occasionally, more than an hour—depending not only on the thickness of the fish, but also on the temperature of your particular cooker, and variations in temperature caused by frequent opening or by outside weather influences.

in an old cake pan or pie pan, but if you do a lot of smoke-cooking you might prefer to buy a steel smokebox at a cooking supply store. This little box has a hinged lid that snaps closed over your wood. Numerous holes top and bottom allow the smoke to circulate. Or you might simply fashion your own "smokebox" out of heavy-duty foil, liberally perforated with a cooking fork. If you use charcoal, wait until the coals are glowing and then cover them with a heavy

SLOW SMOKING

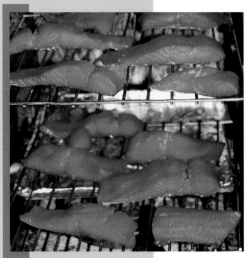

Placed on wire racks, brined fillets cure for several hours in a smoker. Finished product, opposite, has a dark, rich appearance and savory smoke flavor.

Smoke-cooking usually takes an hour or less and produces a moist and tasty main dish for a barbecue party. Slow smoking, on the other hand, produces a delicious dry snack or appetizer that can also be used to make delicious spreads and salads.

A workable fish smoker can be home-made out of such containers as a large metal garbage can, an old refrigerator, a metal ice chest or a discarded wall oven. All you have to do is rig wire racks inside, provide for entrance of air at the bottom of the unit plus a small exit hole at the top, and come up with some source of very low heat. In a safe area, a smoldering hardwood fire inside your smoker can do the job. Or you might use an electric hotplate with a metal pan in which to burn hardwood chips.

But few city folks care to go to all that trouble, especially since small manufactured smokers are widely available at low cost. These work beautifully and take up little storage room in the average household. They need only be placed in a fireplace or patio and plugged in to start working. And one filling of its racks will produce enough smoked fish to please a large family.

You begin by drawing a lot of the moisture from the fish. This is done by soaking the fish for quite a long time in a brine-and-spice solution, after which it is allowed to air-dry and to take on a glaze. Then it is placed in the smoker, on wire racks, and cured for several hours, surrounded in the smoker by smoke and low heat, in the neighborhood of 100 to 180 degrees.

For best preservation results, brining should last about six hours; however, if long shelf life is not your goal—and it seldom is for home smoking—then brining time can be much shorter, maybe only an hour or so. Various spiced-up brining solutions may be used, but the basic one is simply a half-cup of non-iodized salt and a half-cup of sugar or brown sugar, dissolved in two quarts of water.

Fillets make for more satisfactory smoked fish than do steaks, although the latter can certainly be used. Leave the skin on and cut the fillets into pieces small enough to be easily arranged on racks of your smoker. Submerge the fish in the brine solution, using a glass, plastic or earthenware bowl as a container. Place a dinner plate or some other weight atop the fish to keep it all below the surface.

After brining, you should rinse the fish, piece by piece, under cold running water, and lay the pieces on paper towels. Wipe the surface with more towels, and

let the fish dry at room temperature for about an hour, or until a noticeable glaze forms on the surface.

As soon as you begin the air-drying period, plug in your smoker for preheating. When the brined fish takes on its glaze, arrange the pieces on the smoker racks so they are not touching. Place thicker pieces on the lower racks, since that will be the hottest area during smoking time.

The smoking will take about four to six hours, depending on thickness. Smoke is provided by filling a small pan with prepared hickory chips or sawdust and placing it atop the heating unit in the bottom of the smoker. A full pan will burn out in something less than an hour and the pan should be refilled perhaps twice or three times during a six-hour period, but since the smoke has nothing to do with the actual cooking-curing process, you could fill the pan less often or more often, with resulting variations in the amount of "smoky taste."

You should begin checking for doneness after four hours—and less if using thin fillets. The outside should have a dark, rich look to it. But to be doubly sure of doneness, take out a piece and break it. Most urban fish-smokers like the meat to be dry but not tough or stringy.

As you try different types of fish in your smoker, you'll develop your own preferences, but don't be afraid to try any of your favorite kinds. Everything doesn't have to be smoked salmon. Smoked fillets of many other "everyday" fish of fresh and salt water are scrumptious.

If you buy one of the portable home smokers, you'll get detailed instructions not only for fish but for meats and other foods as well.

FISH in LIQUID
Poaching, Steaming

The names are different and so are the procedures—slightly—but both poaching and steaming produce much the same results. The slight difference in treatment is that poached fish is cooked directly in a small amount of liquid, whereas in steaming, it is cooked on a rack above the liquid. Either way, simmering in a closed vessel accomplishes the aim.

In addition to the recipes in this chapter, it should be noted that simple poached fish, without any sauces or embellishments, can be stored for several days in the refrigerator and used to make a great many spur-of-the moment dishes, such as sandwiches and simple salads, that are very low in calories. Check Chapter 9 for some good recipe suggestions, but don't be afraid to add leftover poached fish on impulse to any soup or stew or stuffing you might make. It may provide a surprising zip to the overall product, and it certainly won't be disagreeable.

Steaming and poaching are easily accomplished on both the stove top and in the microwave. Whichever method you employ, be sure to keep cooking time under careful control. Although overcooking is not likely to be as damaging to fish that's cooked in steam, as it is to, say, fried fish, it can definitely make the final result tougher and less tasty.

CHAPTER FIVE

STEAMING AND POACHING TIPS

Oversize steamers that accommodate a large salmon are available in cooking supply stores, but the average household is more likely to poach fillets and steaks using vessels at hand. Smaller salmon and large trout are delicious when poached. So are all the members

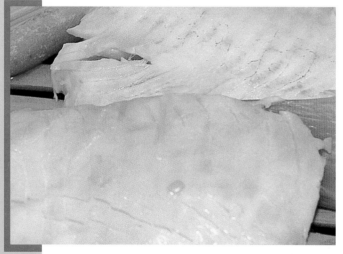

Poached fish is delicate, since it is steamed in salt water or perhaps even court bouillon. Enjoyable both hot and cold.

of the saltwater tuna family. Although lean, white-meat varieties of both fresh and saltwater fish are seldom poached, they are quite tasty when prepared this way—especially when tossed with condiments of your choice and served in a salad.

The procedure is to use a vessel with a lid and in it boil barely enough lightly salted water to cover steaks, fillets or fish chunks about one to two inches thick. Add two teaspoons of vegetable oil or margarine to the water. Place fish gently on the bottom of the vessel or, for steaming, use a rack. Cover and reduce the heat to low. Simmer for eight or 10 minutes, or until fish flakes with a fork. Drain immediately.

A common variation—and a considerably better one—is to poach the fish in court bouillon rather than water.

Plain poached or steamed fish is enjoyable either hot or cold. When a more elaborate presentation is desired, the recipes used are basically for sauces and garnishes that go on the cooked fish.

BOUILLONS

C ourt bouillon is a light broth made by boiling carrots, celery, onion or other vegetables, along with spices and fish stock. This is made at the time of use—never stockpiled in advance. Three of many variations are given here.

BASIC COURT BOUILLON

- ✔ **3 cups water**
- ✔ **1 onion, sliced**
- ✔ **¼ cup vinegar**
- ✔ **½ tsp. salt**
- ✔ **½ tsp. black pepper**
- ✔ **1 bay leaf**
- ✔ **¼ tsp. thyme**

Put all ingredients in pan. Stir. Bring to a boil and simmer at least 30 minutes before cooking fish.

COURT BOUILLON DELUXE

- ✔ **1 cup red wine**
- ✔ **2 cups water**
- ✔ **¼ cup each of carrots, celery and onion, chopped**
- ✔ **2 tbsp. butter**
- ✔ **½ tsp. salt**
- ✔ **½ tsp. black pepper**
- ✔ **½ lemon, sliced**

Sauté the vegetables in the butter until soft, not brown. Add other ingredients and boil 15 minutes before cooking fish.

COURT BOUILLON WITH WINE

- ✔ **2 cups water**
- ✔ **1 cup white wine**
- ✔ **½ tsp. salt**
- ✔ **½ tsp. pepper**
- ✔ **½ lemon, sliced**

Combine all ingredients, bring to a boil, and add fish immediately.

POACHED FISH MEUNIÈRE

1. Poach fish in court bouillon and remove to platter.
2. Sauté scallions in butter. Blend in flour and stir constantly while heating, 3 or 4 minutes. Add milk and stir until smooth. Add salt and wine; simmer 5 minutes more.

Remove from heat and stir in egg yolks. Spoon sauce over fish. Serves 3 or 4.

- ✔ **2 pounds fillet of sole or other mild fish**
- ✔ **Court bouillon**
- ✔ **1 cup scallions, chopped**
- ✔ **½ cup butter**
- ✔ **3 tbsp. flour**
- ✔ **2 cups milk**
- ✔ **½ tsp. salt**
- ✔ **½ cup white wine**
- ✔ **2 egg yolks, beaten**

POACHED FISH HOLLANDAISE

- ✔ **2 pounds fish fillets**
- ✔ **Court bouillon**
- ✔ **Hollandaise sauce**
- ✔ **Lemon slices**

1 Poach fillets in court bouillon, remove to platter and cover with Hollandaise sauce. Garnish with lemon slices.

As to the Hollandaise sauce, you can make your own from scratch or use prepared sauce or a mix. Serves 3 or 4.

POACHED FISH STEAKS WITH CHEESE SAUCE

Swordfish, salmon and tuna lend themselves especially well to this recipe.

Place all ingredients except fish in a large skillet. Bring to boil, then turn down heat and simmer for 15 minutes. Add fish steaks.

Cover and simmer for 10 minutes. Turn steaks and simmer about 5 minutes more. Test for flakiness with fork. Serve with following sauce.

✔ **Fish steak, or steaks, totaling about 2 pounds**
✔ **2 cups beer**
✔ **2 sprigs parsley**
✔ **1 medium onion, sliced**
✔ **1 stalk celery, sliced**
✔ **1 bay leaf**
✔ **2 whole cloves**
✔ **4 peppercorns**
✔ **1 carrot, thinly sliced**

CHEESE SAUCE

✔ **Broth from preceding recipe**
✔ **2 tbsp. butter**
✔ **1 tbsp. flour**
✔ **½ cup milk**
✔ **¼ cup Gruyere cheese**
✔ **¼ cup grated Parmesan cheese**
✔ **1 egg yolk**
✔ **2 tbsp. heavy cream**
✔ **¼ tsp. salt**
✔ **¼ tsp. pepper**

1. Boil broth until reduced to a half-cup. Strain.
2. In a skillet, melt half the butter, add flour and blend well.
3. Bring milk to a boil in a saucepan and then add slowly to butter-flour mixture, stirring constantly until sauce is smooth. Add the strained broth and cheeses and mix gently.
4. In a separate bowl, beat the egg yolk lightly and add a small amount of the hot sauce. Add to mixture and cook over low heat until sauce thickens. Stir in rest of butter, cream and seasonings.

Pour sauce over fish steaks, then place steaks under a hot broiler until lightly browned. Serves 4 or 5.

POACHED FISH WITH MUSHROOMS

- ✔ **2 pounds fish fillets**
- ✔ **Wine-style court bouillon**
- ✔ **1 onion or 2-3 scallions, chopped**
- ✔ **Butter**
- ✔ **small can mushroom slices**
- ✔ **1 can condensed cream of mushroom soup**

1 Poach fish in court bouillon and remove to platter.

2 In skillet, brown onion or scallions in a little butter. Add the mushroom slices and soup. Stir until smooth.

3 Add some of the court bouillon—a little at a time— stirring constantly until desired consistency is obtained. Ordinarily, less than a cup of the court bouillon is used.

Pour sauce over poached fish. Serves 3 or 4.

POACHED FISH WITH OYSTERS

1. Poach fish in court bouillon and remove to platter.
2. Cool one cup of the court bouillon and mix in the well-beaten egg yolk, scallions and lemon juices.

Simmer for 3 minutes, add oysters, and simmer 3 more minutes. Pour over fish and serve. Serves 2 or 3.

- ✔ ½ **pound fish fillets**
- ✔ **Court bouillon**
- ✔ **1 egg yolk**
- ✔ **2 scallions, chopped**
- ✔ **Juice of ¼ lemon**
- ✔ **12 raw oysters**

POACHED TROUT NORMANDY

- ✔ **2 large fillets of trout or salmon, up to 2 pounds each**
- ✔ **Court bouillon**
- ✔ **½ stick butter**
- ✔ **1 onion, chopped**
- ✔ **¼ cup flour**
- ✔ **½ cup white wine**
- ✔ **1 pound boiled shrimp, or 1 can shrimp**
- ✔ **2 hard-boiled eggs**
- ✔ **Salt and pepper to taste**

1 Poach fish in court bouillon and remove to platter, reserving bouillon.

2 Saute the onion in the butter. Blend in the flour. Add one cup of the court bouillon and the wine.

Simmer 5 minutes. Chop shrimp and eggs, and stir lightly into sauce. Pour sauce over fish. Serves 6.

POACHED FISH SUPREME, WITH WINE

- ✔ 1½ pounds salmon steaks or thick, white-meat fillets
- ✔ Fish stock or deluxe court bouillon
- ✔ ½ stick butter
- ✔ 2 scallions, chopped
- ✔ ¼ cup flour
- ✔ ½ tsp. each, salt and pepper
- ✔ 1 egg yolk
- ✔ ½ cup white wine
- ✔ 2 cups mashed potatoes, prepared and seasoned

1 Poach fish in bouillon or stock and remove to platter, reserving liquid.

2 Sauté scallions in butter and sprinkle in the flour, blending well. Blend in 2 cups of the fish stock or court bouillon, salt and pepper. Heat until steaming but not boiling.

3 Beat egg yolk and wine together and stir into the hot sauce. Remove from heat.

Make a ridge of mashed potatoes all around the fish on the platter. Pour sauce over fish and place under hot broiler until potatoes start to brown. Remove and serve immediately. Serves 3 or 4.

FISH
IN THE
MICROWAVE

I n modern-day kitchens, the microwave oven is as common an appliance as a toaster. Unfortunately, all too many people use their microwaves for jobs no more glamorous than baking a potato or heating a cup of water. That's a shame, because nearly any culinary goal can be tastily achieved with a microwave—and achieved much faster than with most other heat sources.

Be advised, however, that when it comes to microwaving fish, faster doesn't necessarily mean better. You can turn out many delicious fish dishes in jig time, but you have to be especially careful on two counts or you might just as easily produce a complete flop.

One area of caution is timing. The biggest pitfall in all of fish cookery is overcooking, and since the microwave cooks so exceedingly fast, just an extra minute, or even half a minute, might spell failure, leaving the fish dry and chewy instead of tender and tempting. The timing problem is made all the more difficult by the fact that microwave ovens differ so much in power, hence in cooking time needed.

MICROWAVING TIPS

To be a successful microwave cook, especially of fish, you generally have to go through a trial-and-error period with your own appliance. Lacking any such advance study, the best way to proceed is to undercut the lowest time suggested in any fish recipe by about one-third. Then stop and do the fork test. If the fish isn't yet done, continue cooking and testing in 30-second increments. After you find the right time for your chosen recipe, be sure to write it down. Practice makes perfect and you will soon learn just how long to cook all the pet dishes that you make with any frequency.

The other drawback is merely aesthetic but certainly important. The microwave will never give you that lovely golden brown look that is developed in a skillet, on a grill or in a conventional oven. You can atone for this shortcoming to some extent by sprinkling your fish with paprika or other colorful seasonings and spices.

One type of fish cookery for which the microwave is especially handy is steaming or poaching (see preceding chapter). The first thing anyone learns about a microwave oven is that it's great for heating water. It follows, then, that it will make a terrific tool for poaching or steaming fish. Plastic microwave steamers are available on houseware shelves, and can just as easily be jury-rigged from a variety of covered plastic containers or glass casseroles found in most kitchens.

It's doubtful that any cook need be reminded to keep metal pans out of the microwave.

Microwave cooking is quick and easy, compared with regular stoves, and is standard equipment on many bigger boats. There's no quicker way to cook up a chunk of fish while trolling offshore, than with one of these ovens. Watch that plate, though, they do get hot.

FESTIVE MICROWAVE FISH

- ✔ **2 skinless fillets**
- ✔ **½ small onion, chopped**
- ✔ **¼ green bell pepper, chopped**
- ✔ **6 or 7 grape tomatoes, halved lengthwise**
- ✔ **4 small mushrooms, sliced**
- ✔ **Salt and pepper**
- ✔ **Garlic powder**
- ✔ **Melted butter or olive oil (or spray oil)**

Cod, tilapia, walleye and other mild, white fish are excellent for this treatment.

1 Place fillets in shallow microwave casserole. Brush or spray with olive oil or butter. Sprinkle with salt, pepper and garlic powder.

2 Arrange chopped vegetables over top. Cook on high for about 3 minutes. Turn halfway and cook on high for 2 additional minutes. Check with fork. Cook another minute or so, if necessary. Serves 2.

CURRIED FISH FILLETS

1. Arrange fish in microwave-safe dish, with thickest parts to outside. Sprinkle with lemon juice, salt and pepper.

2. Cover with plastic wrap and cook on high for 3 minutes. Turn dish 90 degrees and microwave 3 minutes longer, until fish flakes with fork.

Remove and let stand while preparing sauce as follows: in a ceramic or glass cup, melt the butter, add flour and curry powder and stir until well blended. Add milk and stir briskly.

Microwave on high at 1-minute increments, stirring after each minute until sauce is smooth and thick. Pour sauce over fish and sprinkle with parsley. Serves 2.

✔ **½ pound fish fillets, cut into serving size pieces**

✔ **1 tbsp. lemon juice**

✔ **Salt and pepper**

✔ **½ tbsp. butter**

✔ **½ tbsp. flour**

✔ **¼ tsp. curry powder**

✔ **¼ cup milk**

✔ **1 tbsp. chopped parsley**

MUSHROOM-PARMESAN MICROWAVE

- ✔ **1 pound fish fillets**
- ✔ **4 ounces mushrooms**
- ✔ **¼ cup onions**
- ✔ **1 tbsp. butter**
- ✔ **½ tsp. salt & pepper**
- ✔ **½ cup sour cream, room temperature**
- ✔ **3 tbsp. Parmesan cheese**

1 Sauté onions until light brown. Add mushrooms and sauté for two minutes more.

2 Arrange fish in a microwave dish with the thickest part in the middle. Spread mixture on top and microwave for 3 minutes on high.

3 Stir Parmesan cheese into sour cream and pour over fish. Sprinkle with bread crumbs and paprika.

Cook on high for about 3 minutes more. Let stand for 2 minutes. Serves 4.

DIJON DELIGHT

- ✔ 1½ pounds fish fillets (flounder, sole, cod, etc.)
- ✔ ½ cup Dijon-style mustard
- ✔ Salt and pepper to taste
- ✔ 2 medium-size tomatoes, sliced
- ✔ 2 zucchini, sliced (optional)
- ✔ ½ teaspoon basil

Place fish fillets in single layer in 13 x 9-inch microwave-safe baking dish. Spread a little mustard on each fillet, sprinkle with salt and pepper, and cover with tomato and zucchini slices. Sprinkle with basil.

Cover with vented plastic wrap and microwave on high for about 6 minutes until fish flakes easily. Serves 6.

MARDI GRAS SPECIAL

- ✔ ½ cup skim milk
- ✔ 2 tbsp. lemon juice
- ✔ 4 firm white fish fillets
- ✔ ¼ tsp. black pepper
- ✔ ¼ cup chopped onions
- ✔ ¾ cup low-fat sour cream
- ✔ 2 tbsp. chopped fresh parsley
- ✔ 2 tbsp. chopped pimentos
- ✔ 1 tsp. Worcestershire sauce
- ✔ 2 dashes Tabasco sauce
- ✔ ¼ cup grated Parmesan cheese
- ✔ 1 pinch paprika

1. Soak fish in milk/lemon juice for at least 30 minutes.
2. Place fish fillets in microwave casserole, thickest portions to the outside.
3. Cover and microwave 3 minutes per pound at 100 percent power or until fish flakes. Drain liquid that remains.
4. In 2-cup microwave measure, cook onion, covered, for 1 minute at 100% power. Stir in sour cream, parsley, pimento, Worcestershire sauce and Tabasco sauce.
5. Top fish with sour cream sauce. Heat at 50% power for 8-15 minutes until very hot, but not boiling. Sprinkle with Parmesan and paprika. Serves 4.

MICROWAVE SALMON JULIENNE

1 Pat fish dry with paper towels and set aside. Cut carrots and potato into julienne strips. Peel, seed and chop tomato.

2 In shallow microwave-proof casserole or gratin dish just large enough to hold everything, arrange fennel, carrots and potatoes. Sprinkle with chopped tomato, onion, 1 teaspoon parsley and basil.

3 Dot with butter. Cover with plastic wrap and microwave on high for 6 or 7 minutes, stirring once, until vegetables are just tender.

4 Arrange fish steaks over vegetables and season lightly with salt, pepper and remaining parsley. Cover with plastic wrap and microwave on high, turning dish a half turn once, for 4 minutes per pound (500 g), or until fish flakes with a fork. Garnish with lemon wedges. Serves 2.

✔ **2 salmon steaks**
✔ **2 carrots**
✔ **1 large unpeeled potato**
✔ **1 large tomato**
✔ **1 cup julienne strips of fennel or celery**
✔ **1 onion, chopped**
✔ **2 tsp. chopped fresh parsley**
✔ **1 tsp. chopped fresh basil**
✔ **2 tbsp. butter**
✔ **Salt**
✔ **Freshly ground pepper**
✔ **1 lemon, cut in wedges**

MICROWAVE DILL-YOGURT TROUT

- ✔ 4 trout, cleaned
- ✔ 1 tbsp. butter
- ✔ 1 cup slivered almonds
- ✔ 1 tbsp. celery seeds
- ✔ ½ tbsp. chopped dill
- ✔ Salt
- ✔ Freshly ground black pepper
- ✔ 2 tsp. cornstarch
- ✔ ½ cup natural yogurt

1 Cook the butter, almonds and celery seeds in a shallow dish for 6 minutes on high, pausing to stir at intervals until the almonds start to brown.

2 Using half the chopped dill, sprinkle a little inside each trout, along with salt and pepper.

3 Arrange the fish head to tail in a shallow dish and cook on high about 6 minutes until the fish is done, turning halfway through cooking. Set aside.

4 Mix the cornstarch with a little yogurt in a small bowl and then stir in the remaining yogurt.

Cook on high for 2 minutes, whisking frequently until thickened. Stir in remaining dill. Serve the trout with the sauce and garnish with the browned almonds. Serves 4.

CAJUN MICROWAVE CATFISH

1. Mix mayonnaise and spices. Coat fish on both sides with mayonnaise mixture and roll in cracker crumbs.

2. Arrange fish on microwave rack or in casserole, thickest portions to the outside.

Microwave on high power (100 percent) for 3-4 minutes. Let stand a few seconds and check for doneness. Fish will flake easily when done.

For added color, sprinkle with paprika (for mild) or Cajun seasoning (for spicier). Serves 4.

- ✔ **1 pound catfish fillets (or other mild fish)**
- ✔ **¼ cup mayonnaise**
- ✔ **¼ tsp. crushed red pepper**
- ✔ **½ tsp. ground cumin**
- ✔ **¼ tsp. onion powder**
- ✔ **¼ tsp. garlic powder**
- ✔ **½ cup crushed crackers**
- ✔ **Cajun seasoning or paprika**

FIESTA MICROWAVE FISH

- ✔ **2 small fillets of white, mild fish**
- ✔ **Salt and pepper**
- ✔ **Garlic powder**
- ✔ **¼ cup chopped onion**
- ✔ **¼ cup chopped green pepper**
- ✔ **1 small tomato, chopped**
- ✔ **6 small or 2 large mushrooms, chopped**
- ✔ **1 cup cheddar cheese, shredded**

Place fish in shallow microwave casserole. Sprinkle with salt, pepper and garlic powder. Spread vegetables over top of fish.

Cook on high for 3 minutes. Turn dish 90 degrees and cook 2 more minutes. Sprinkle cheddar cheese over fish and cook 2 more minutes, or until cheese melts. Serves 2.

ORANGE MICROWAVE FISH

Place each fillet in a microwave safe dish. Melt the butter in a cup or small bowl. Stir in the orange juice, zest and dill.

Cover dish with plastic wrap and cook on high for about 2 minutes. Turn dish 90 degrees and cook an additional 2 minutes or so. Let stand another minute and test for doneness with fork. Garnish with orange and cucumber slices. Serves 2.

✔ **2 fish fillets**
✔ **1 tbsp. butter**
✔ **Juice and zest of ½ orange**
✔ **1 tsp. chopped dill**
✔ **Orange slices for garnish**
✔ **Cucumber slices for garnish (optional)**

FISH IN THE STEWPOT

Chowders, Soups, Stews

Many fish soups are thick, but thick or thin, they are generally referred to as chowders. Some, though, may wear the label "stew." A hungry chef-fisherman and his guests aren't likely to quibble over the terminology, because one thing most of these concoctions have in common is that a generous bowlful, along with some bread and perhaps a salad, makes for a hearty meal.

One reason for the popularity of chowders is that they are easily put together in camp or on any boat large enough to sport a galley or pack an alcohol stove. Catch a fish, fillet it, and boil it up with some onion, salt and potato (instant potato works fine), and you're ready to chow down. Of course other additives, such as pepper, milk, tomatoes, butter, bacon or additional seasonings would brighten up the basic dish.

Chowders are commonly but informally divided into two groups—the Manhattan type, built around a tomato base, and New England, founded on milk or cream. But those are far from the only good variations of fish soups, as you'll see in this chapter.

CHAPTER SEVEN

NEW ENGLAND CHOWDER

- ✔ **2 pounds fish**
- ✔ **Salt pork**
- ✔ **3 large potatoes, diced**
- ✔ **1 large onion, sliced**
- ✔ **2 cups milk, cream or half-and-half**
- ✔ **Butter, salt and pepper**

1 Cut fish into small pieces. Simmer in a saucepan with barely enough water to cover.

2 Fry a small piece of salt pork in a skillet. Add diced potatoes and toss. When potatoes are brown, add them and the sliced onion to the fish. Simmer a few minutes until potatoes and fish are tender.

3 Add milk or cream, and heat to verge of boiling. Add a large pat of butter. Remove and serve. Individuals should salt and pepper their servings to taste. Serves 6.

MANHATTAN CHOWDER

1 Cut fish into small pieces. Fry bacon until lightly brown and crisp. Add onion, green pepper and celery.

2 Cook until tender. Add rest of ingredients and simmer for about 20 minutes until potatoes are tender. Serves 4.

✔ 1 pound fish
✔ 2 slices bacon or equivalent salt pork
✔ 1 small onion, chopped
✔ ½ green pepper, chopped
✔ 1 cup celery, chopped
✔ 1 cup fish stock or chicken broth
✔ 1 large potato, diced
✔ 1 tsp. salt
✔ 1 large can tomatoes
✔ ½ tsp. pepper

FAST FISH STEW

- ✔ 1 pound fish fillet
- ✔ 1 medium onion, chopped
- ✔ One 1-pound can tomatoes
- ✔ 1 large potato, diced
- ✔ One 1-pound can mixed vegetables
- ✔ ½ cup water
- ✔ ¼ tsp. salt

1 Simmer all ingredients except fish and mixed vegetables together for 20 minutes.

2 Add fish and vegetables (including liquid from vegetables) and simmer 15 minutes longer.

3 With long-handled spoon stir mixture well, breaking fish into small pieces. Serves 4.

FAST CHOWDER FOR CAMP OR HOME

- ✔ 1 pound fish
- ✔ 4 medium potatoes
- ✔ 1 small onion
- ✔ 1 can evaporated milk
- ✔ 2 tbsp. butter or margarine
- ✔ Salt and pepper

1 Cut potatoes in half and put into saucepan with the sliced onion and the fish. Barely cover with water and boil gently until potatoes are soft when pierced with a fork.

2 Use a large spoon to coarsely mash the fish and potatoes.

3 Stir in a can of evaporated milk and heat to verge of boiling. Add butter. Salt and pepper to taste, individually. Serves 4.

QUICK MUSHROOM CHOWDER

1 In a skillet, sauté the mushrooms in butter until tender. Add fish and cook about five minutes, breaking fish apart with fork when tender.

2 Combine soup with milk and heat separately, stirring until smooth and hot, but not boiling.

3 Add contents of skillet to soup. Stir in pimento and sherry. Add salt and pepper to taste. Serves 6.

- ✔ 1 pound fish fillets
- ✔ ½ pound mushrooms, sliced
- ✔ 4 tbsp. butter
- ✔ 2 cans condensed cream of mushroom soup
- ✔ ½ cup milk
- ✔ 2 tbsp. chopped pimento
- ✔ 2 tbsp. sherry
- ✔ Salt and pepper

ONION FISH SOUP SUPREME

- ✔ **1 pound uncooked fish, cut into small pieces**
- ✔ **3 slices bacon, diced**
- ✔ **6 large onions, sliced**
- ✔ **1 stick butter**
- ✔ **2 tbsp. Wondra flour**
- ✔ **2 chicken bouillon cubes**
- ✔ **4 cups boiling water**
- ✔ **½ cup grated Swiss cheese**
- ✔ **Salt and pepper**

1 Fry bacon in a Dutch oven. Add onions, butter and seasonings and cook until onions are soft. Sprinkle with Wondra and stir until smooth.

2 Add boiling water to pan gradually while stirring constantly. Add bouillon cubes and continue to stir until dissolved.

3 Add fish and simmer 10 minutes. Serve in bowls with cheese sprinkled over top. Use any kind of natural cheese you like. Serves 6.

EUROPEAN CHOWDER

✔ **2 pounds fish**
✔ **¼ stick butter**
✔ **1 carrot, diced**
✔ **1 onion, sliced or chopped**
✔ **1 tsp. salt**
✔ **Generous sprinkling of black pepper**
✔ **1 cup white wine**

1. Melt butter in skillet and brown fish, which need not be cooked through.

2. If you use a Dutch oven, proceed in the same vessel; otherwise, transfer fish to saucepan, add other ingredients, bring to boil and boil gently for 5 minutes—or longer if carrot is not tender.

3. There is no danger of too much boiling, so unless you're pressed for time, simmer another 15 minutes. Add the juice of ½ lemon (optional), stir and serve.

CATFISH STEW, SOUTHERN STYLE

- ✔ **1 pound skinned catfish fillets**
- ✔ **2 slices bacon**
- ✔ **1 large onion, chopped**
- ✔ **1 large can tomatoes**
- ✔ **½ cup green pepper, diced**
- ✔ **2 large potatoes, diced**
- ✔ **1 tsp. salt**
- ✔ **1 cup boiling water**
- ✔ **2 tbsp. Worcestershire sauce**
- ✔ **¼ cup ketchup**
- ✔ **¼ tsp. thyme**

1 In Dutch oven or heavy saucepan, fry bacon, remove, drain on paper and crumble back into pan with the chopped onion.

2 Brown onion lightly; then add water, tomatoes and other ingredients except fish.

3 Simmer for 30 minutes, covered. Add fish, cut into bite-size pieces, and simmer 15 more minutes, uncovered. Serves 4.

NEW YORK STEW

- ✔ 1½ pounds cod, halibut or other white fish
- ✔ ½ cup celery, diced
- ✔ 1 small onion, chopped
- ✔ 1 carrot, chopped
- ✔ 1 large potato, diced
- ✔ ½ tsp. garlic salt
- ✔ Flour for thickening
- ✔ ½ cup (small can) shrimp or crabmeat (optional)

1 Place vegetables in saucepan, barely cover with water, and boil for 15 minutes.

2 Add fish and garlic salt, along with shrimp or crab (if you like), and simmer another 10 minutes.

Thicken with flour paste, if necessary. Stir to break up fish and to mix well. Serves 4 or 5.

DELUXE STEW

- ✔ **2 pounds fish**
- ✔ **1 onion, sliced**
- ✔ **1 cup white wine**
- ✔ **1 cup mushrooms, sliced**
- ✔ **1 large potato, diced**
- ✔ **¼ tsp. thyme**
- ✔ **1 small carrot, thinly sliced**
- ✔ **½ cup celery, chopped**
- ✔ **Generous sprinkling of salt and pepper**

1 Sauté fish lightly in a little oil or butter. Add onion slices and brown. Add wine and other ingredients.

2 Cover and simmer about 15 minutes, or until vegetables are tender. Stir lightly to break up fish, and thicken with flour paste, if desired. Serves 6.

HASHHOUSE CHOWDER

1 In a large saucepan or, preferably, a Dutch oven, sauté the onion and celery in butter over medium heat, until transparent.

2 Add frozen vegetables, water and fish and simmer until tender, about 15 minutes. Add milk and tomato sauce.

3 Thicken with cornstarch. Salt and pepper to taste. Bring just to boiling point and serve immediately. Serves 4.

✔ 1 pound fish fillets, cut into bite-size pieces
✔ 1 pkg. frozen mixed vegetables
✔ ½ stick butter
✔ 1 small onion, chopped
✔ ½ cup celery, chopped
✔ 1¼ cups water
✔ 2 cups milk
✔ 2 tbsp. tomato sauce
✔ 2 tbsp. cornstarch
✔ Salt and pepper

QUICK BOUILLABAISSE

- ✔ 1 fish, about 3 or 4 pounds live weight
- ✔ ½ stick butter
- ✔ 1 onion, minced
- ✔ 1 clove garlic, minced
- ✔ 1 bay leaf
- ✔ 2 cloves
- ✔ 1 tsp. salt
- ✔ ½ tsp. black pepper
- ✔ 1 cup fish or chicken stock
- ✔ 1 small can tomatoes
- ✔ 1 can shrimp
- ✔ 1 can baby clams

1 Scale and fillet fish, retaining head, skin and bones. Boil all parts except fillets in enough water to cover, for 20 minutes. Strain.

2 In a large frying pan, sauté onion and garlic, then brown fish fillets. Add other ingredients and stock, and simmer for 15 minutes.

This dish can be spiced up by adding ¼ cup of sherry and a tablespoon of Worcestershire sauce. Serves 4.

FRENCH BOUILLABAISSE

1 In a large pan or Dutch oven, sauté the onion and garlic in the butter. Add fish and other seafood (except clams) and sauté about 5 minutes until seafood is cooked.

2 Add stock, clams and other ingredients and simmer 10 more minutes.

Serve by spooning portions of each seafood into bowls, then ladling liquid into each bowl. Float a lemon slice on top. Serves 6.

- ✔ 2 pounds fish fillets
- ✔ 1 doz. large shrimp, peeled and veined
- ✔ 1 doz. oysters
- ✔ 1 pound lobster meat
- ✔ 6 small scallops
- ✔ 6 clams in shell
- ✔ ½ cup butter
- ✔ 1 large onion, minced
- ✔ 1 garlic clove, minced
- ✔ 2 cups fish stock (made from head and bones)
- ✔ 1 large ripe tomato, peeled
- ✔ 1 tsp. salt
- ✔ 1 lemon, sliced
- ✔ ¼ cup red wine

FISH FROM THE FRIDGE
Leftover Fish, Flaked Fish

Flaked fish, whether left from yesterday's dinner or fresh and quickly cooked by boiling or microwaving, can be used to prepare many tasty and out-of-the-ordinary meals. If the fish is left over, it makes little difference whether it is fried, boiled, baked or poached. If it's fried, you might, for aesthetic reasons, wish to remove as much of the cold coating as possible before flaking, but either way, it will have no effect on the taste of these recipes and very little on the appearance.

Actually, you can often do without a recipe, for cold fish is a tasty addition to many "standard" salads, and it also makes wonderful sandwiches. Some special sandwich treatments are described in this chapter, but you should also note that plain cold fish, combined with lettuce, tomato and mayonnaise, ranks right alongside cold turkey in "sandwich appeal."

CHAPTER EIGHT

FISH RAREBIT

- ✔ **2 cups flaked fish**
- ✔ **1 tbsp. butter or margarine**
- ✔ **2 tbsp. flour**
- ✔ **1 cup milk**
- ✔ **½ cup grated cheddar cheese**
- ✔ **1 small can mushrooms, drained**
- ✔ **1 tsp. chili sauce**
- ✔ **2 drops Louisiana hot sauce**
- ✔ **Salt**

1 In a saucepan over medium heat, melt butter and blend in flour and a dash of salt. Add milk gradually, stirring and heating until thick. Stir in cheese.

2 When melted, add chili sauce and hot sauce. Stir in flaked fish and mushrooms. Heat and serve over toast or rice. Serves 2 or 3.

MacFISH SALAD

- ✔ 2 cups flaked fish
- ✔ 3 cups cooked elbow macaroni
- ✔ ½ cup chopped green pepper
- ✔ ½ cup chopped onion
- ✔ 2 tbsp. wine vinegar
- ✔ ½ cup mayonnaise
- ✔ 1 tsp. spicy mustard
- ✔ 2 hard-boiled eggs, sliced
- ✔ 4 slices bacon, fried crisp

1 After frying bacon, mix one tablespoon bacon grease with the vinegar, mayonnaise and mustard. If bacon grease clumps, heat the mixture and allow to cool.

2 Mix the other ingredients except eggs and bacon. Stir in the dressing. Arrange sliced eggs over top and sprinkle with crumbled bacon. Serves 4.

POTLUCK SEAFOOD SALAD

- ✔ 1 cup flaked fish
- ✔ 1 small can crabmeat
- ✔ 1 small can shrimp
- ✔ 1 cup celery, chopped
- ✔ ¼ cup cucumber, sliced thin
- ✔ 2 tbsp. lemon juice
- ✔ ½ cup mayonnaise
- ✔ 6 strips pimento
- ✔ Salt and pepper

Toss all ingredients well. Chill and serve on lettuce in small bowls or cocktail cups. Salt and pepper to taste. Add a small strip of pimento to each serving for color. Serves 6.

CAESAR NEPTUNE SALAD

Toss all ingredients well. Chill thoroughly. Serve on romaine or lettuce. Serves 6.

- ✔ **2 cups flaked fish**
- ✔ **1 can green peas**
- ✔ **1 cup ripe olives, chopped**
- ✔ **1 cup celery, chopped**
- ✔ **1 small green pepper, chopped**
- ✔ **1 bottle Caesar salad dressing**

SHRIMPY FISH SALAD

- ✔ **1 pound flaked fish**
- ✔ **1 cup shrimp, chopped**
- ✔ **2 tbsp. lemon juice**
- ✔ **½ cup celery, chopped fine**
- ✔ **1 tsp. dill weed**
- ✔ **½ cup mayonnaise**
- ✔ **3 hard-boiled eggs, quartered**
- ✔ **Salt and pepper**

1 Combine fish and shrimp and toss lightly with lemon juice. Add celery, mayonnaise, onion and dill. Salt and pepper to taste. Chill.

2 Arrange on a bed of lettuce with quartered eggs as garnish, along with several whole shrimp, if available. Serves 6.

FRUITY FISH SALAD

Combine all ingredients in a two-quart bowl. Toss lightly and serve on lettuce leaves. Serves 4.

- ✔ **2 cups flaked fish**
- ✔ **1 apple, chopped**
- ✔ **1 banana, sliced**
- ✔ **One 8-ounce can pineapple chunks, drained**
- ✔ **½ cup raisins**
- ✔ **½ cup chopped pecans or walnuts**
- ✔ **½ cup mayonnaise**
- ✔ **1 tbsp. lemon juice**

FISH AND MUSHROOM SALAD

- ✔ **1 cup flaked fish**
- ✔ **2 cups sliced fresh mushrooms**
- ✔ **1 cup julienne-cut Gruyere cheese**
- ✔ **¼ cup chopped parsley**
- ✔ **3 tbsp. olive oil**
- ✔ **½ tsp. salt**
- ✔ **¼ tsp. pepper**

Toss all ingredients and serve in individual salad bowls on lettuce or other greens, with blue cheese dressing on the side. Serves 4.

TOMATOES STUFFED WITH FISH

- ✔ **1 pound flaked fish**
- ✔ **6 medium tomatoes, ripe but firm**
- ✔ **1 cup cracker crumbs**
- ✔ **1¼ tsp. seasoned salt**
- ✔ **½ tsp. dill weed**
- ✔ **½ cup celery, chopped**
- ✔ **¾ cup mayonnaise**
- ✔ **½ tsp. lemon juice**

1 Cut a slice from the stem end of each tomato and scoop out the pulp and seeds. Drain tomatoes well.

2 Combine all ingredients and fill tomato shells. Chill, then serve on a bed of lettuce. Serves 6.

AVOCADO STUFFED WITH FISH

- ✔ 1½ cups cooked fish, flaked
- ✔ ½ cup celery, diced
- ✔ ¼ cup cooked green peas
- ✔ ¼ cup mayonnaise
- ✔ 2 tbsp. sugar
- ✔ 2 tsp. lemon juice
- ✔ ½ tsp. curry powder
- ✔ ½ tsp. salt
- ✔ ¼ tsp. pepper
- ✔ 2 ripe avocados, cut in half and pitted

Blend mayonnaise, sugar, seasonings and lemon juice. Toss together fish, celery and peas. Blend all lightly and use to stuff four avocado halves.

SHARP FISH SANDWICHES

1. Cut rolls in half, butter and brown lightly under broiler.

2. Combine other ingredients. Divide and spoon the mixture on six halves of rolls.

3. Top each with a slice of cheese. Place under broiler until cheese is barely melted. Serve as is or top with remaining halves of rolls.

- ✔ 2 cups flaked fish
- ✔ ½ cup celery, chopped fine
- ✔ ¼ cup onion, chopped fine (optional)
- ✔ 1 cup grated sharp cheddar cheese
- ✔ 6 slices sharp cheddar cheese
- ✔ ¼ cup sweet pickle relish
- ✔ ½ cup mayonnaise
- ✔ 6 egg rolls or hamburger buns

SUNNY FISH SANDWICHES

- ✔ 1½ cups flaked fish
- ✔ 1 cup sliced almonds
- ✔ ½ cup chopped celery
- ✔ ½ cup mayonnaise
- ✔ 2 tbsp. lemon juice
- ✔ 12 English muffin halves, toasted and buttered
- ✔ 24 cooked or canned asparagus spears
- ✔ 6 slices American cheese
- ✔ Paprika

1. Combine fish, almonds, celery, mayonnaise and lemon juice.

2. Arrange muffin halves on a cookie sheet. Place two asparagus spears on each muffin half. Cover asparagus and muffin with about ⅓ cup of fish mixture.

3. Cut each slice of cheese diagonally into quarters. Place two cheese triangles on each sandwich.

4. Sprinkle with paprika and bake at 400 degrees for about 15 minutes until cheese melts and sandwiches are heated. Serves 6.

CREAMY FLAKED FISH CASSEROLE

- ✔ **2 cups flaked fish**
- ✔ **½ tsp. salt**
- ✔ **2 tbsp. lemon juice**
- ✔ **1 tbsp. butter**
- ✔ **1 can condensed tomato soup**
- ✔ **2 cups mashed potatoes**

1 Mix fish with salt and lemon juice. Add butter (no water) to soup and heat, stirring until smooth. Do not boil. Add fish and mix.

2 Pour into shallow casserole or baking dish. Top with mashed potatoes. Place under broiler for a few minutes until potatoes brown. Serves 6.

FISH FIESTA CASSEROLE

- ✔ **2 cups flaked cooked fish**
- ✔ **1 can cheddar cheese soup**
- ✔ **½ cup milk**
- ✔ **One 4-oz. can green chilies, chopped and seeded**
- ✔ **¼ cup chopped onion**
- ✔ **1½ cups broken tortilla chips**

1 Combine soup, milk, chilies and onion in a bowl.

2 Add fish and one cup of chips. Stir lightly and pour into a one-quart casserole (or four ramekins).

3 Top with remaining chips. Bake at 400 degrees for 30 minutes. Serves 4.

BAKED FISH LOAF

- ✔ **2 cups flaked fish**
- ✔ **1 chicken bouillon cube**
- ✔ **1 cup boiling water**
- ✔ **½ cup bread cubes**
- ✔ **2 eggs, beaten**
- ✔ **½ cup celery, chopped**
- ✔ **½ cup milk or light cream**
- ✔ **1 tsp. onion, grated**
- ✔ **1 tsp. salt**
- ✔ **2 tsp. lemon juice**

1 Put bouillon cube in water and stir until cube dissolves. Add all other ingredients, mix well, and place in a greased loaf pan.

2 Bake at 350 degrees for about an hour, or until loaf is firm in the center. Serves 6.

CREAMED FISH

- ✔ 2 cups flaked fish
- ✔ ½ pound mushrooms, sliced
- ✔ ½ stick butter
- ✔ 2½ cups milk
- ✔ 3 tbsp. cornstarch
- ✔ ½ cup cold water
- ✔ 1 small onion, chopped
- ✔ Salt and pepper
- ✔ Pimento strips for color

1 Sauté the onion and mushrooms in the butter over medium heat. Pour in milk and heat barely to boiling.

2 Mix water with cornstarch and add for thickening. Stir in flaked fish. Salt and pepper to taste. Warm well. Serve on toast or rice. Serves 4.

FISH NEWBURG

- ✔ **2 cups flaked fish**
- ✔ **2 egg yolks**
- ✔ **1 tbsp. cornstarch**
- ✔ **1½ cups milk or light cream**
- ✔ **Salt and pepper**
- ✔ **Dash of nutmeg**
- ✔ **2 tbsp. butter**
- ✔ **4 tbsp. sherry**
- ✔ **Paprika**

1. Beat egg yolks with cornstarch until light. Gradually add milk, stirring constantly.
2. Put into top of double boiler (or use a chafing dish) with the fish. Add light dashes of salt, pepper and nutmeg.
3. Cook over briskly boiling water until sauce is quite thick. Add butter and sherry and stir.
4. If desired, sprinkle with paprika for a touch of color. Serve on rice or toast. Serves 5 or 6.

CHEESY FISH CASSEROLE

1 In a saucepan, cook onion in 2 tbsp. butter until clear. Stir in flour and salt and a sprinkle of pepper. Add one cup of the milk. Cook, stirring, until thick and bubbling.

2 Remove from heat, add cheese and stir until melted. Use remaining half-cup of milk to prepare cream sauce according to instructions on package.

3 Stir cheese mixture, peas and mushrooms into sauce. Stir in flaked fish. Divide into six one-cup individual ramekins.

4 Melt 2 tbsp. butter and toss with bread crumbs. Sprinkle crumbs on casseroles. Bake at 400 degrees for 15 minutes. Serves 6.

✔ **1 pound leftover fish, flaked**
✔ **¼ cup onion**
✔ **4 tbsp. butter**
✔ **2 tbsp. flour**
✔ **¼ tsp. salt**
✔ **Pepper**
✔ **1½ cups milk**
✔ **1 cup shredded American cheese**
✔ **1 envelope White Sauce mix**
✔ **1 cup frozen peas, thawed**
✔ **1 small can mushroom pieces**
✔ **1½ cups soft bread crumbs**

FISH QUICHE

- ✔ 1 cup flaked, cooked fish
- ✔ One 9-inch pie crust
- ✔ 3 eggs, beaten
- ✔ 1½ cups milk
- ✔ 1 tbsp. flour
- ✔ 1 tsp. Worcestershire sauce
- ✔ 1 tsp. prepared mustard
- ✔ 1 dash Tabasco sauce
- ✔ ½ cup Swiss cheese, shredded
- ✔ ½ cup Gruyere cheese, shredded
- ✔ ¼ tsp. salt

1 Prepare pie crust and line a nine-inch dish. Line crust with two thicknesses of heavy foil and bake five minutes at 450 degrees.

2 Remove foil and bake five minutes more, or until crust is light brown. Remove crust from oven and reduce heat to 325 degrees.

3 In bowl combine eggs, milk, flour, Worcestershire sauce, mustard, Tabasco and salt.

4 Sprinkle flaked fish over pie crust. Pour mixture over fish and sprinkle with cheeses.

Bake at 325 degrees for 45 minutes.

NOTE: Edges of crust may be covered with foil to prevent overcooking. Allow to cool 15 minutes before serving. Serves 6.

FISH AND MUSHROOM PIE

1. Prepare pastry mix and line a pie pan.
2. Fry bacon until crisp; drain. To scalded milk add onion and salt. Add the hot milk slowly to beaten eggs, stirring constantly.
3. Spread fish over pie shell. Spread mushrooms over fish. Pour in the milk-egg mixture, and sprinkle crumbled bacon over the top.
4. Bake in 425-degree oven for 20 minutes. Reduce heat to 325 and bake about 15 minutes longer until pie is firm in center. Serves 6 or 8.

- ✔ 2 cups flaked fish
- ✔ 1 cup pastry mix
- ✔ 3 slices bacon
- ✔ 1¼ cups milk, scalded
- ✔ 1 tsp. onion, grated
- ✔ ½ tsp. salt
- ✔ 3 eggs, beaten
- ✔ 1 can mushrooms, drained (4 oz.)

FISH for NIBBLING
Appetizers

Fish—other than sashimi (read "raw') and processed types such as anchovies and sardines—are not often seen on the hors d'oeuvres table. Here are a few home preparations that will tastily remedy that oversight.

Sushi recipes and treatments make up a specialized culinary topic too intricate to be included in this book, but sushi's bar-mate, sashimi, is simplicity itself, being essentially any raw fish sliced thin and served with various "dips" such as soy sauce, tempura sauce or wasabi. The one recipe in this chapter that has "sashimi" in its name is really only a hybrid; it's partially cooked.

There is also a Latin American favorite called Seviche that seems raw at first glance but is actually very well cooked—not on a fire but by being marinated in lime juice. If you don't believe lime juice can substitute for fire, look closely at the finished fish. It's white. Raw fish would be opaque. And a quick taste will confirm that it's "cooked."

Seviche is served either as a first-course seafood cocktail, or as a snack with cold beer. And speaking of fire, the chili peppers and Tabasco sauce listed in the recipe may be left out by the timid or increased by the bold.

CHAPTER NINE

SEVICHE

- ✓ **1 pound white meat fish, cut in bite-size pieces**
- ✓ **1 large onion, chopped or sliced**
- ✓ **1 tomato, chopped fine (remove seeds)**
- ✓ **1 small green pepper, chopped fine**
- ✓ **2 chili peppers, chopped fine**
- ✓ **Tabasco sauce, a liberal sprinkling**
- ✓ **Juice of 4 to 6 limes (lemons can be substituted)**
- ✓ **Salt**

If you plan to serve your seviche the same day, proceed as follows:

1. Salt the pieces of fish liberally and stack them loosely in a crock or glass container.
2. Add the other ingredients, stir well, and add fresh-squeezed lime juice to cover.
3. Marinate for a few hours until all pieces are white, with no pinkish centers.

As an appetizer, this serves 6 or 8. Serves fewer when offered as a snack with crackers and drinks.

A slightly different approach is needed if you plan to store your seviche in the refrigerator for nibbling over the next few days. In that case, do not include the other ingredients but simply marinate the salted fish in lime juice until it turns white. After marinating, drain off the lime juice (this prevents further "cooking"), add the chopped vegetables and other ingredients, and mix well. Seviche prepared in this manner will stay firm and tasty in the fridge for several days.

SEMI-SASHIMI

- ✔ Fresh tuna steak
- ✔ Salt
- ✔ Garlic powder

PONZU SAUCE

- ✔ 1 cup orange juice
- ✔ ½ cup sake
- ✔ ¼ cup sugar
- ✔ ¼ cup soy sauce
- ✔ ¼ teaspoon dried crushed red pepper
- ✔ 2 teaspoons water
- ✔ 1½ teaspoons cornstarch

Combine orange juice, sake, sugar, soy sauce and red pepper in heavy, small saucepan. Boil and reduce to medium heat for about 5 minutes. Dissolve cornstarch in water and stir until smooth, add to boiling mixture and stir constantly until sauce thickens. Makes about a cup.

1 Use only fresh or vacuum-sealed frozen tuna of highest quality.

2 Sprinkle salt and garlic powder over all surfaces. Rub or spray the steak with oil or butter and sear it quickly—no more than a minute per side—in a preheated and very hot iron skillet.

3 Remove steak to a cutting board and slice thinly with a sharp knife. Serve with Japanese dipping sauces, or even plain soy sauce, but anyone who relishes rare tuna steak or beefsteak may prefer to wolf it down without further adornment.

A recipe for one traditional sauce is at right.

SEASHELL DELIGHTS

- ✔ **2 cups flaked cooked fish**
- ✔ **1 medium onion**
- ✔ **1 small green pepper, chopped fine**
- ✔ **1 cup celery, chopped fine**
- ✔ **1 cup buttered bread crumbs**
- ✔ **1 cup mayonnaise**
- ✔ **1 tsp. Worcestershire sauce**
- ✔ **Parmesan cheese, grated**
- ✔ **Salt and pepper**

Use seashell (scallop shell) halves, or imitations purchased at kitchen supply shop. Crab meat or chopped shrimp may be mixed with (or substituted for) the fish.

1 Grease well with butter. Mix all ingredients except bread crumbs and cheese.

2 Divide mixture and place on shells. Sprinkle with bread crumbs and Parmesan. Lightly salt and pepper.

3 Bake at 350 degrees until lightly browned, about 30 minutes. Serves 6 or 7.

PARTY PATTIES

✔ 2 cups flaked fish
✔ 2 eggs, lightly beaten
✔ ½ cup ketchup
✔ 1 cup crushed saltines
✔ 1 small onion, minced

For breading:
✔ 1 egg, well beaten
✔ ½ cup flour

Patties can be made in advance and held covered in refrigerator for several hours or overnight.

1 Stir together first set of ingredients. Shape into balls or patties. Dip each ball into beaten egg and then into flour, coating well.

2 Fry quickly in deep fat at 375 degrees for about one minute or until browned. Serves 4.

REGAL ROUNDS

✔ 1½ cups flaked fish
✔ ¼ pound pimento cheese
✔ ¼ cup chopped nuts
✔ ¼ cup sweet relish
✔ ¼ cup crushed pineapple
✔ ¾ cup grated coconut

1 Make two complementing snacks by first mixing the fish with the soft cheese.

2 To half that mixture add chopped nuts; to the other half add relish and pineapple. Form small balls and roll each ball in coconut. Chill.

SMOKED FISH SPREAD

- ✔ **1½ pounds smoked fish**
- ✔ **2 tsp. minced onion**
- ✔ **2 tsp. celery, chopped fine**
- ✔ **1 clove garlic, minced**
- ✔ **2 tbsp. sweet pickle relish**
- ✔ **1 cup mayonnaise**
- ✔ **1 tbsp. mustard**
- ✔ **½ tsp. Worcestershire sauce**

Flake the fish and stir all ingredients together thoroughly. Chill well before serving on crackers. Makes about 3 cups.

To turn this tasty spread into a dip, take a portion of it and thin to desired consistency by slowly stirring in some sour cream.

SMOKED FISH DIP

Break up fish well with fork. Mix all ingredients in blender or food processor. Serve with assorted crackers and raw vegetables.

- ✔ **1 pound smoked fish**
- ✔ **One 8-ounce package whipped cream cheese**
- ✔ **1 pint sour cream**
- ✔ **1 tsp. prepared mustard**
- ✔ **3 tbsp. lime juice**
- ✔ **3 tbsp. chopped celery**
- ✔ **3 tbsp. sweet pickle relish**
- ✔ **3 tbsp. finely chopped onion**
- ✔ **2 tbsp. mayonnaise**

FISH in PREPARATION
Cleaning, Wrapping, Freezing

Perhaps cleaning fish will never be looked upon as one of man's great recreational delights, but with most fish it really isn't a great challenge.

The first thing you must do, of course, is decide just how you want to dress your catch. Usually there are options, and although the main call should be based on the way you plan to cook your fish, other factors can enter into your decision—for instance, how tired you are, or how much time you want to devote. A nice five-pound bass or snapper would look great on the table after it has been scaled, dressed and baked. But then, you're sun-burned and it would be so-o-o much quicker just to slice off the fillets.

No matter your final decision, the task will be easier if your catch has been kept on ice and is by now thoroughly chilled. Fish that go straight from a livewell to the cleaning table are not very good prospects for fast, neat cleaning.

Fish-cleaning duty becomes far less objectionable if three basic rules are followed: (1) keep the right tools handy; (2) clean the fish in a place selected for maximum ease and convenience; (3) familiarize yourself with any of the different cleaning techniques you're likely to need—and practice them.

CLEANING YOUR CATCH

The electric fillet knife at right will come in handy for that fine smallmouth bass just landed, above.

Okay, so cleaning fish is no one's favorite chore. Having caught them makes the job more tolerable however, since we're fulfilling that hunting and gathering instinct that goes way back in history.

It's best to learn cleaning skills early and with the right tools; wasting part of the catch certainly isn't right. Sometimes, with a little effort, you can even find folks who will take the head and bones for fish soup stock.

Often the only tool needed is a knife, but it must be a good one—and sharp. Traditionally, the most useful all-around tool has been a thin fillet knife with a 6-inch blade. However, an electric knife with power (now provided at dockside cleaning tables by many marinas and fishing camps) is a powerful friend, when you're confronted with a pile of fish that need cleaning. Rechargeable electric knives, along with 12-volt models that plug into the cigarette lighter of your boat or car, can certainly come to the rescue in places where there is no electricity or convenient plug.

As for traditional knives, many models are available, and with stainless blades they range in price from a few dollars to out-of-sight, the really expensive ones being hand-crafted. Just any good knife won't do for efficient filleting. While some kitchen knives may look similar, a proper fillet knife has a blade that is thinner and not so rigid as, say, a boning knife. Opinions vary among anglers as to just how flexible a filleting blade should be, but some degree of flexibility is a must.

The most common blade length for fillet knives is six inches. Four-inch blades (or pocket knives) will be needed at times for dressing panfish, and 8 or 9-inch blades are the ticket for saltwater anglers who sometimes have to tangle with bigger catches.

It's advisable to keep one 6-inch fillet knife in your tackle kit, and an identical one at home. And it's not a bad idea to keep two in the tackle box. That's in case your fishing buddy, at cleaning time, announces that he's "forgotten" to bring along a knife of his own. Think how pleased he'll be when you graciously offer him the use of your spare! (The spare may also be needed if someone decides to chip block ice with your favorite, flexible blade.)

Other cleaning tools that may come in handy (depending on where you fish and for what) are a fish scaler and a pair of pliers. And it almost goes without saying that a sharpening tool should always be close at hand for manual blades. Again, try to keep one in your tackle box and another at home, for those times when you're unable to clean your fish on the water.

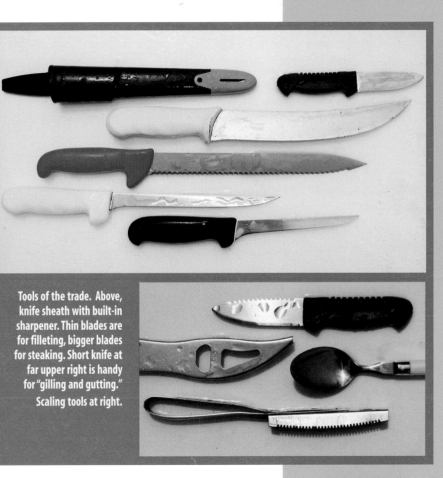

Tools of the trade. Above, knife sheath with built-in sharpener. Thin blades are for filleting, bigger blades for steaking. Short knife at far upper right is handy for "gilling and gutting." Scaling tools at right.

Fish-cleaning chores left to young angler. Fortunately, those Spanish mackerel are easy to fillet.

clean fish on location than to bring them home and do it. Fish scales fly hither and yon as you scrape them off, and your spouse may take a dim view of scales speckling the kitchen. Also, there is a disposal problem in the average city home. Even if you have woods in your back yard for burying fish carcasses, they're usually dug up by varmints and sometimes left in odd places, like your neighbor's yard or under your house.

But if you must dress your fish at home, here are some hints that should help:

When scaling, hold the fish under water in the sink, so the scales won't fly about. Then, for gutting and beheading, place numerous layers of newspaper on a counter top. As the mess grows, keep wrapping it in a few layers of paper and setting it aside. This not only avoids a single big pile of garbage, but also provides you with a new and clean surface from time to time as you go along. When you're filleting instead of dressing and scaling, place the pad of newspaper sheets atop a cutting board and, again, wrap the refuse at intervals as you find necessary.

As each fish (or fillet) leaves the cleaning surface, it should be placed, without rinsing, in a dry sink or dry, clean pail. Wait until the entire job is finished, before you rinse all the dressed fish under cold running water and then immediately prepare them for cold-storing or freezing.

Obviously, you could drag your tools out of the tackle box for home cleaning, which would be perfectly all right, so long as you're the infallible type who always remembers to put them back. But cleaning fish at home should basically be avoided if at all possible. A waterside table saves as much time and effort as the right tools. Most marinas and fish camps provide fish-cleaning facilities, a table or wooden surface of the appropriate height, complete with handy water supply. But even without those, you'll normally find it easier to

CLEANING FISH THE RIGHT WAY

Several factors must be considered in determining how you wish to dress your fish. One of them, obviously, is size. You wouldn't try to stuff and bake an average-size bluegill. The selected method of cooking is another important consideration. When you bring home a 4-pound bass, say, or a nice striper, or a fat snapper, you'll have a decision to make: *Should you prepare the fish whole for baking, or remove the fillets for frying or broiling?*

Such fish as large salmon and king mackerel are often steaked, but smaller ones of the same species can be either steaked or filleted, according to your own preference. Once you make a choice as to the end product desired, proceed with the task of dressing, as described in the illustrated instructions that follow.

DRESSING PANFISH

"Panfish" is a catchall term for any edible fish, whether from fresh water or the sea, a fish so small that it is normally cooked nearly whole. Naturally, the entrails must be removed, and usually, but not always, the head is lopped off as well. Some people prefer to leave the head on for visual appeal; others maybe because there are a few bites of exceptionally tasty meat in the "cheeks" of many varieties. If the head is not removed, the gills should be cut out. The majority of panfish also require scaling, but with a few—such as small freshwater trout and saltwater pompano, scales are either non-existent or small enough to be ignored. The list of edible fish in this book makes note of those kinds that need no scaling, but if any doubt persists, it really won't hurt any of them to undergo a scraping.

WHOLE PANFISH

1 Cut off the head. Some like to cut the pectoral fins off with it, as shown. Others prefer to cut closer behind the gills and leave the pectorals. Remove the entrails.

2 A fish-scaling tool is good, but a knife or even a spoon can also be used to remove the scales.

Pay attention to the spots that might be overlooked if you get in too big a hurry.

Panfish now ready for the pan. The dorsal and anal fins could be cut out, but this takes considerably more time and is not really necessary, because the fins are easily pulled off after cooking.

PREPARING LARGE FISH FOR BAKING

Procedures for dressing a large fish that you plan to bake are essentially the same as for panfish. But it's a bigger job, and one that will require more effort and more elbow room. In addition to scaling and eviscerating the fish, you may wish to remove the dorsal and anal fins as well, because this will eliminate many small bones at the top of the fish.

If the fins are removed, simply slicing them off at the surface serves no purpose except to make the fish look a little neater—while adding to the bone problem. As a final step, you may also cut off the tail, but there is no real reason to do so unless it doesn't fit your pan. Many cooks leave as is.

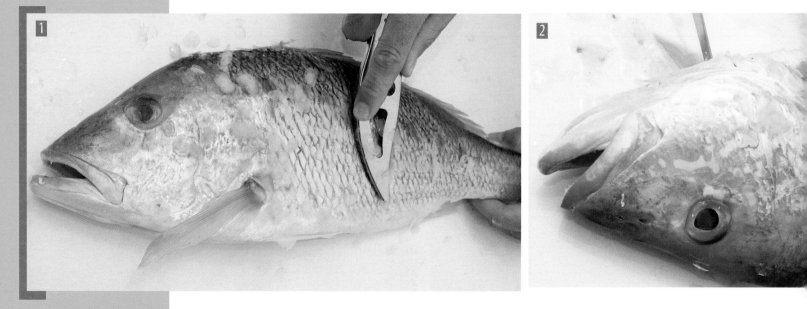

WHOLE LARGE FISH

1 The first step is to scale the fish. This can be a pretty tough job with many species. Again, my preferred tool is the scaler, although a sturdy table-spoon will do the trick. As with panfish, take care that all scales are removed from dorsal and belly surfaces, as well as from the sides.

2 Some like to leave the head on for dramatic effect. If you prefer to do so, be sure to cut out the gills. Now, after drawing the entrails, the fish should be ready. But you will have less trouble with bones if you remove the dorsal and anal fins before cooking.

3 Slit the belly from vent to throat and remove the entrails. The dorsal and anal fins can be left on and pulled out after cooking, but you will have far less trouble with bones if you remove the fins now.

OPTIONAL FIN REMOVAL:

Keeping knife flat, make a rather deep cut the length of the dorsal fin. Turn fish and make the same cut along the other side of the dorsal.

Using the knife to help grip, grasp the dorsal fin at the tail end and pull firmly upward and toward the head end. Remove the smaller anal fin on the underside the same way.

Your fish is now ready for baking. Just avoid the rib cage when serving and the meat will be bone-free.

STEAKING

In fish-eating language, a "steak" usually means a slice cut from the dressed carcass of a whole fish, with a segment of backbone included. However, the term is also applied to slices cut from the boneless fillets of very large fish, such as swordfish. Steaks vary in thickness from a minimum of about a half-inch to as much as two inches. The average is around three quarters of an inch.

When should a fish be steaked rather than filleted? There's no rigid rule on this, but these tips may help you decide.

(1) Follow custom. Many market fish—halibut, large salmon, king mackerel and swordfish among them—are usually sold as steaks. Anglers, therefore, often follow the same custom with their own catches.

(2) Appearance. You may just like the looks of a broiled fish steak on your plate better than a fillet, or partial fillet, cut from the same fish.

(3) Variable size capability. You can slice fish steaks to preferred thickness—using thin steaks for quick cooking or fatter ones for slower cooking methods, especially with recipes that include sauces or special trimmings.

(4) The most common reason for steaking is simply that the particular fish is too large to make filleting practical. But in this case, of course, you have a good option: Instead of steaking the entire "log" of the fish, you can cut the thick fillets from both sides of the backbone and then cut half-size steaks from the fillets.

Beautiful wahoo landed in a tournament, ready for steaking. With bigger fish, round steaks may be too large (in diameter) and need to be trimmed or halved.

WHOLE FISH STEAKS

1 To prepare a whole fish for steaking you can essentially follow the same instructions as for preparing a baking fish. The first step is scaling—if necessary. This step can be eliminated with members of the mackerel and tuna families. Next, eviscerate the fish.

2 Cut off the head. Again, it's your choice as to whether or not to remove the dorsal and anal fins. Fish markets generally leave them intact, both to save labor and to keep each steak more attractive. If you cut out the fins before steaking, the steaks will be virtually free of tiny, troublesome bones.

3 Steaking a fish is almost like thick-slicing a loaf of bread. They can be joined in the middle but split at the top, and some of them at the bottom too—not so pretty but less bony.

With the carcass lying on a cutting board, make a straight-down cut, very much like slicing a loaf of bread. Of course, there is no backbone in a loaf of bread, and the spine may cause

you some trouble, depending on the size of your fish, its species and what tools you have.

Sometimes, with fairly small or soft-boned fish, your knife will slice right through the bone with little effort—and with big fish too, if you happen to hit between the vertebrae. If the bone resists your knife, don't struggle. Simply cut through the flesh until you hit the bone, then take care of the bone with a kitchen saw, frozen food knife or a cleaver. Or, if your knife is thick-bladed and sturdy, you can hammer it through.

Each round-shaped steak is a meal in itself and cooks fast over an open grill.

HOW TO FILLET AND SKIN

This is the easiest and fastest of all fish-cleaning methods, and one that's suitable for the great majority of catches, large or small. The product is a slab of boneless meat from each side of the fish. The scales are most often removed with the skin but, if you prefer, you can scale the fish before filleting it and leave the skin on. That's up to you.

Many fishermen may never think of filleting any fish under, say, one pound in weight, but many others routinely fillet their larger bluegills or species that normally are treated as whole panfish. The fillets will be quite small, of course, but if you have a great enough catch to feed the number of people you have in mind, they are delicious and, best of all, boneless.

Exceptionally large bluegills or other sunfish that are caught from still or muddy water may have a strong "musky" flavor, much like that of largemouth bass from the same water. Filleting and skinning will remove the flavor, most of which can be traced to fat just under the skin.

Choice red snapper and seabass ready for the fillet knife. Notice how well these fish are iced down to keep fresh and tasty.

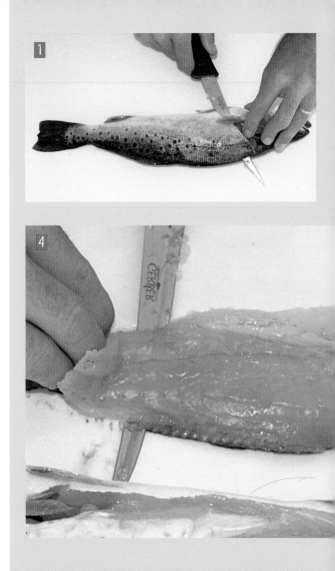

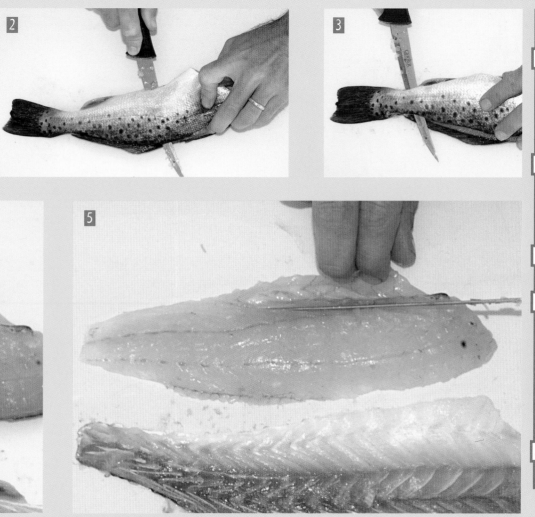

BASIC FILLET TIPS

1 Place the whole fish on a firm surface, and with a sharp, fairly flexible fillet knife, make a cut behind the pectoral fin down to the backbone. If you make a straight vertical cut, the rib cage will come off with the fillet; a diagonal cut around the rib cage will leave the ribs on the backbone.

2 To remove fillet, turn the knife until its blade lies flat against the backbone. Work the cutting edge toward the tail with a slight sawing or pushing motion (depending how sharp the knife is) slicing through the rib cage and removing the entire fillet.

3 Leave tail skin connecting fish to fillet. If not, you'll have to grip the skin yourself for the next step.

4 To separate the skin, hold the tail end of the fillet down snugly and work the knife forward until the blade lies nearly flat between skin and flesh, but with the edge angled slightly downward. Too much of a downward angle and you may cut through the skin, too much upward and you may lose meat. With the tail pinned, work the knife forward, pulling on the skin with the other hand. Little if any meat should be left attached to the skin.

5 The final step is to remove rib bones from fillet. Simply slice away any rib cage.

FILLETING LARGE FISH

1. For large fish like this grouper, it's far more practical to make a cut around the fillet before cutting inside. A sharp knife is essential here. Take your time and watch that hand. Wearing a glove on that bare hand will save nicks and cuts, when you've got a pile of fish to clean.

2. Make long, shallow cuts, scraping just over the backbone, gradually peeling the meat back.

3. Keep cutting and peeling, avoiding large bones in the backbone. Avoid the rib cage, if you prefer.

4. This fillet is already missing the rib cage, left inside the fish. (It can also be sliced off the fillet at this point).

5. Last step is to pin the fillet down, and remove the skin. A thin and flexible blade is preferable here.

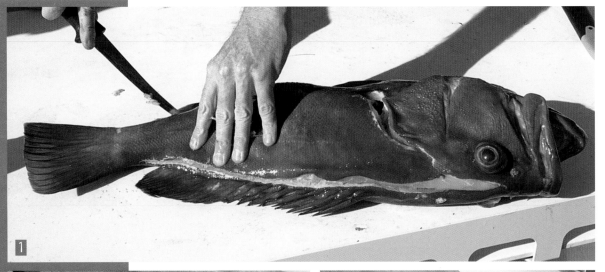

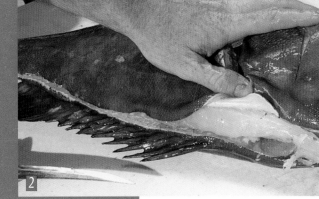

FILLETING WITH ELECTRIC KNIFE

Electric knifes are a blessing and make the job of filleting mid-sized fish a real breeze. In experienced hands, a pile of fish becomes a bag of fillets in only a few minutes.

1) Starting just behind the gill plates, cut down until you touch the backbone, then turn 90 degrees toward the tail. Stop just short of the tail, and flip the fillet away from the fish.

2) The tail skin remains connected. This provides an easy grip, with the other hand far from the knife. Skin the fillet, leaving skin attached to fish.

3) Skinless fillet then has its rib cage trimmed off.

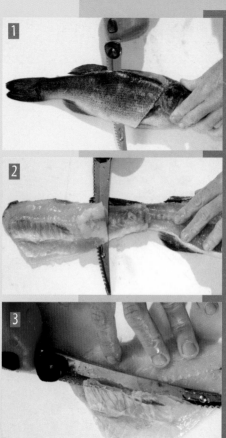

FILLETING FLOUNDER

Flounder are a special fish, and cleaning them is somewhat different. Many anglers prefer to bake them whole, but filleting is not that difficult, with a little practice.

1. The fish is cut around the dark (and thicker side) first.

2. Next, start on one side and keep peeling the meat back with a thin, sharp fillet knife.

3. Fillet is separated from fish.

4. Skinning is the same as any other fish fillet.

5. Fillet can be separated down the middle and trimmed into tasty fingers for frying.

Bottom, or white, side of large flounder also can be filleted.

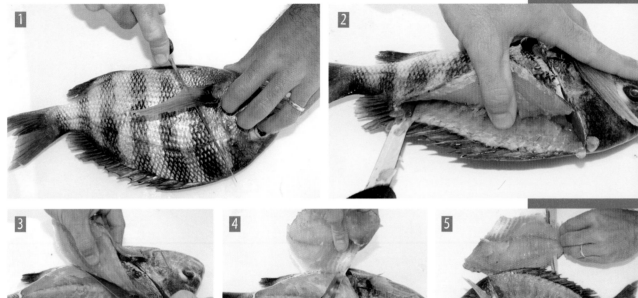

FILLETING SHEEPSHEAD

Sheepshead, members of the porgy family, are easier to clean than many believe, and quite tasty on the plate.

1. Make the standard cut under the pectoral fin, stopping at the thick backbone.

2. At the top of the fish, peel back the meat just above the ribs. Once past the big rib cage, push the blade all the way through, then separate fillet at the tail.

3. Holding fillet, cut backwards toward the head.

4. Knife should ride just over the rib cage, leaving it intact inside fish.

5. Separated fillet is very easy to skin.

THE BUTTERFLY FILLET

A "butterfly" fillet, or double fillet, is achieved by leaving the two sides of your fish—scaled, not skinned—attached at the belly. There are several common uses for a butterfly fillet, but the most popular is for stuffing and baking. You layer the stuffing of choice atop one side and then fold the other side over it and bake. The same thing could be done with two separate fillets, and often is, but the hinged fillet makes for a more attractive presentation. Also, the double fillet leaves the skin intact, and this helps improve the baked product by holding in juices.

1 After optional scaling, cut off the head just behind the pectoral fin.

2 Starting at the head end, position the knife flat against the backbone and cut toward the rear—slicing through the rib bones but taking care not to cut through the skin on the belly.

3 When you reach the vent, push the point of the knife through the bottom skin and finish cutting off the fillet to the tail.

4 Turn fish over and cut off the other fillet. This time you'll probably find it easier to start at the tail end. Cut through from top to bottom until you reach the vent, then make sure the knife point stays inside the chest cavity while you cut through the ribs and complete the filleting.

5 This is the double fillet, ready for stuffing and baking. After discarding the entrails, the backbone may also be kept, if you like.

SKINNING CATFISH

Catfish have skin instead of scales, so they're different to clean. Catfish anglers prefer the nail-and-board scenario, instead of a cleaning table.

1 Stabilize catfish by impaling head on nail.

2 Outline the fillet with a thin blade, cutting barely through the skin.

3 With pliers or gripping tool, get a grip on skin and begin to pull toward tail.

4 Pull skin off tail and discard. Repeat on other side.

Cut off head, remove entrails and fry entire body. Bigger catfish should be cut into finger-size chunks.

PREPARING FISH FOR THE FREEZER

Ziploc bags are good, but for longer freezer life, try using heavier tupper-ware-style plastics. As for aluminum foil, use it for cooking, not freezing.

When properly packaged and stored in a true zero-degree freezer, many kinds of fish can be kept for a year or longer and still taste fresh when served.

The best results in long-term freezing are provided by species that have white meat with few or no red or dark streaks. Examples include freshwater bass and panfish, saltwater grouper, rockfish, flounder and

many others. Oily fishes, such as mackerel, bluefish, mullet and salmon, are not good candidates for long freezer life. Even when frozen with water in a sealed bag or container, or frozen in a heavy, vacuum-sealed plastic bag, they will enjoy, at best, only about half the freezer life of the white-meat fishes.

Nearly every cook knows that fish (and other foods too) should be kept as air-tight as possible when frozen, in order to avoid the drying out called "freezer burn." Dried spots are not harmful, but the dried areas themselves are tough and tasteless, and when you see spots of freezer-burn, you can be almost sure that the rest of the fish will have, at best, an "unfresh" taste.

When freezing fish in water, using a plastic or metal container, drop the pieces loosely into the container. Do not pack them tightly but allow enough room at the top so that water can cover all the fish and still leave space for expansion of the ice as it freezes. Fill the container with water from the cold tap. Let it sit a few seconds until all air bubbles disappear, then add more water, if necessary, to reach the desired level—about a half-inch below the lip. Now all that's left is to affix the lid and freeze. Use a felt marker to write the contents and the date of freezing on the lid.

If using bags, place the pieces of fish inside and fill

the bag with water to the very top, then seal the bag with a twist-tie, or zip it closed.

Good temporary results can be obtained by freezing your fish in a plastic bag without water but with the air removed. To accomplish this, immerse the filled bag in water, leaving only the mouth of the bag exposed. Then tie the bag off just below the water line with a twist-tie. Water pressure will have forced out the air.

Any whole fish, large steak, or other configuration too big to fit a container must, of course, be wrapped separately for freezing. By far the best wrapping material is heavy-duty freezer paper, plastic-coated on one side.

To wrap fish properly, tear off a piece of freezer paper large enough to cover the length and breadth with considerable overlap. Place the fish on the slick side of the paper and proceed as shown in the illustrations by bringing the sides together atop the fish and folding down several times until snug.

After you have wrapped the ends, seal them with tape.

A grease pencil can be used to mark paper or foil, so long as the surface is not wet. Some felt markers will not work on a damp surface.

THE THREE BEST WAYS TO ACHIEVE AN AIR-TIGHT PACK ARE, IN ORDER OF LONG FREEZER LIFE:

(1) sealing in heavy plastic bags with a vacuum machine (longer than a year)

(2) freezing in water (up to a year)

(3) freezing in a plastic bag or heavy wrapping paper from which air has been manually removed (two or three months)

Handy vacuum machine in the kitchen helps remove harmful air from fish fillet, avoiding later freezer burn.

FOOD FISH of NORTH AMERICA

With Cleaning and Cooking Suggestions

This section is designed to answer some common questions such as, "Is this fish good to eat?" or my favorite, "How should I cook it?"

These listings cover all the major hook-and-line food fish of North America, both fresh water and salt water, with notes on table quality, best methods of dressing and preferred methods for cooking.

Take note that subjective comments on taste—comments such as "Excellent," "Fair," or "Poor"—are deliberately avoided here. While it's true that most anglers and fish-lovers do have preferences, it is just as true that any fish worth the trouble of cleaning can be made quite tasty. The few that should be avoided are noted.

Where closely related species are involved, comment for all are under a single heading: for instance the trouts, basses, and groupers. Because only prominent members are illustrated, this section should not be taken as a complete identification manual but only a cooking guide.

Hundreds of additional illustrations and guidance are in the author's five best-selling "Sport Fish of…" book series. See the back pages of this book.

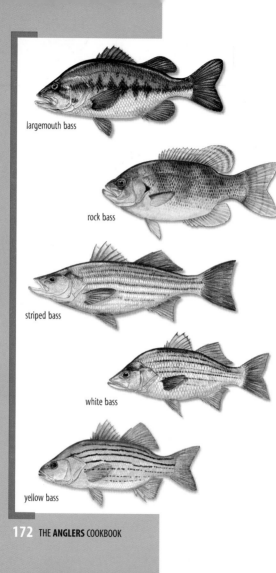

largemouth bass

rock bass

striped bass

white bass

yellow bass

FRESHWATER FISH

BASS, BLACK This group includes the largemouth and smallmouth bass, plus several closely related species such as the spotted or Kentucky bass, redeye bass, Suwannee and Guadalupe bass. All can be treated alike. The largemouth is widely regarded as the poorest eating of the lot, but this isn't necessarily so. The largemouth does often have a "muddy" odor and taste, particularly if taken in still, mud-bottomed waters. Since smallmouth and the other species are usually taken in clear or flowing waters, this odd taste is encountered only in rare, large specimens, and is never pronounced even then. In defense of the largemouth, however, it is unlikely you'll notice any difference between species of similar size caught in similar waters. And, in any event, a largemouth bass that is filleted and skinned loses the objectionable taste. Bass meat is white, firm and lean. Large specimens are inclined to coarseness, another good reason to release them. Fish of one pound and up should be filleted and skinned. Smaller fish can also be scaled and baked whole, but watch out for that muddy taste if a big largemouth is prepared in the same way.

BASS, ROCK This name is widely used for the striped bass. However, the freshwater rock bass is another species entirely, similar to the warmouth and usually prepared as panfish.

BASS, STRIPED The saltwater striped bass is now an introduced staple in many freshwater lakes. It's also called rock bass, rockfish or simply "rock." The meat is firm and white, suitable for any of the preparation methods you might prefer. The fish can be scaled and filleted, or skinned and filleted, even prepared whole.

BASS, WHITE This is a close relative of the striped bass, and is good but ranks below the striper in table quality. It can be treated as striped bass, but is usually of panfish size and should be so handled. Larger ones can be scaled and filleted or skinned and filleted.

BASS, YELLOW Another related species, it is treated as for white bass.

CARP Small specimens can be quite good and lend themselves to a variety of cooking methods. Carp of any size should be skinned. Large ones are coarse, but good when the meat is boiled and then ground or flaked, and used in chowders or as ground fish for fish cakes and similar uses. Hugely popular in the Orient.

CATFISH This is a large family and although most are referred to as types of catfish, you'll also hear other names, such as "bullhead" and "pout." Some types, such as the channel catfish and blue catfish, have better table reputations than others, but all are excellent eating. All catfish should be skinned. Best of all are the little fellows, deep-fried whole. Catfish of between one and six pounds should be filleted after skinning, and the fillets cut into the proper-size pieces for frying, or for chowder. Serving-size pieces cut from big catfish can be fried, but you'll probably like them better in chowders or stews, or baked with sauces.

DRUM Also called sheepshead or gaspergou, this fellow is inclined to coarseness. Small ones are pretty good when scaled and baked. Others should be skinned and the meat used for chowder.

GRAYLING Though not related, the grayling usually is thought of in connection with trout. That association extends to the dining department. They are handled and prepared similarly to pan-sized trout, although the scales are larger and best scraped off. In taste appeal they are at least equal to trout, and many anglers like them better. They can be pan-fried, poached or broiled.

MUSKELLUNGE Muskies make fine eating but, like other top-level gamefish are usually released these days. Since even a "small" keeper muskie is big, many are baked, with or without stuffing. Though the scales are small in comparison to the size of the fish, some folks like to scrape them before drawing and preparing, although this is optional. The muskie can also be filleted (and skinned if you prefer), then cut into small pieces for frying or broiling.

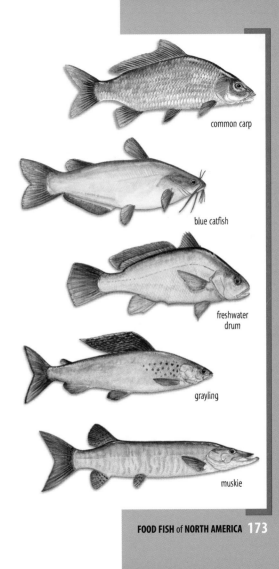

common carp

blue catfish

freshwater drum

grayling

muskie

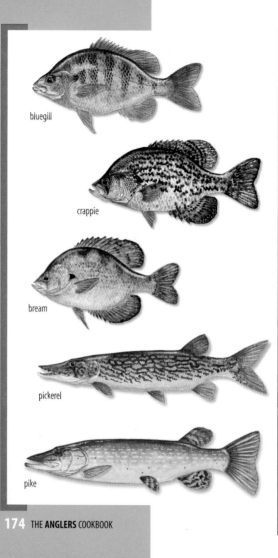

bluegill

crappie

bream

pickerel

pike

FRESHWATER FISH

PANFISH A lot of different small, freshwater fish are lumped together here—all of the sunfish family (including bluegill, called "bream" in the South), plus crappies, perch and the smaller basses. All are excellent food fish and prepared the same way, although you can easily tell a difference in the taste of, say, a crappie and a bluegill. After cleaning, they are most commonly fried in deep fat, but can just as easily be pan-fried or broiled. Bluegills, shellcrackers and other sunfish, along with rock bass and warmouth, sometimes develop a "muddy" taste, especially when they reach sizes approaching a pound and are taken from still or murky water. If you do notice a disagreeable taste in your larger panfish, it can be removed simply by skinning the fish. Also, when frying larger panfish whole, some folks prefer to score each side two or three times. This allows the thicker portions to become properly cooked in a short time.

PICKEREL Although unbelievably bony, chain pickerel are delicious, the meat fine and white. In larger members of this family—the pike and muskellunge—the myriad bones are large enough to be picked out. This is almost an impossible job with the pickerel. Try this: Fillet the pickerel, leaving the skin on; lay skin side down on a cutting board, and with a sharp knife slash the meat of each fillet many times, close together, from one end of the fillet to the other. Do not cut through the skin (some cuts through the skin can't be avoided and are okay, so long as the fillet holds together). Now cut each fillet into serving-size pieces and deep-fry them. The bones will have been cut even smaller, and further softened by frying. They can be eaten along with the meat. Pickerel have very small scales which are hard to scrape off, so many people don't bother to do so. The small redfin pickerel can be scored on the sides and deep-fried whole, as panfish.

PIKE, NORTHERN This fish is very bony, as are its relatives, the muskie and pickerel. For specimens up to seven or eight pounds, follow directions given for pickerel. Big ones can be treated as muskie, since the bones are large enough to be picked out—which can be a demanding job, but not impossible and certainly worthwhile.

SALMON This group includes the Atlantic salmon of the North Atlantic and its rivers; landlocked salmon and ouananiche salmon, which are strictly freshwater strains of the Atlantic salmon; and any of those same varieties, including the king and coho, which have been introduced to the Great Lakes. In their prime, all salmon are famous food fish, and arguments concerning which species are best are mostly opinion. But note that phrase "in their prime." This means fish taken from the sea (or lakes), and stream fish in the early stages of their spawning runs. The longer salmon stay in a stream, the more their flesh deteriorates. But the change in flesh quality is obvious to the eye. Because of this, nobody is apt to get stuck with a bad salmon on the table. Salmon have small scales that are usually ignored, but can be scraped off if you like. The fish then generally is steaked and either broiled, baked or poached. Whole salmon of appropriate size may also be baked or poached in a large steaming vessel. For smoking, salmon should be filleted. Poached salmon may be eaten hot with lemon or a mild sauce, or cold with mayonnaise or another sauce of your choice.

SAUGER Often confused with the walleye, the confusion is appropriate when dinner time arrives. The sauger is equally delicious (better, say some), with fine, sweet flesh. Often skinned, they can also be scaled and filleted without skinning, then fried or broiled. Or you can bake a whole dressed sauger.

SHAD Most of the raves go to the roe of this fish, but the flesh can also be a gourmet's delight, if you get rid of those bothersome bones. If you wish to bake your shad, use the butterfly fillet. Bone each fillet individually, then fold the two fillets back together with stuffing in between. For broiled shad, the fillets can be cut off separately and boned. In any case, scale and behead the shad first. The skin should not be removed. There are several species of shad in North America; all are good if large enough, the larger the better. The common shad, which is the subject of most angling attention, averages three or four pounds.

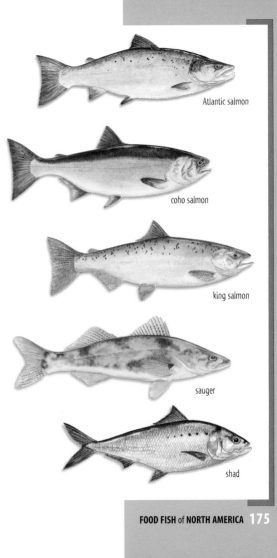

Atlantic salmon

coho salmon

king salmon

sauger

shad

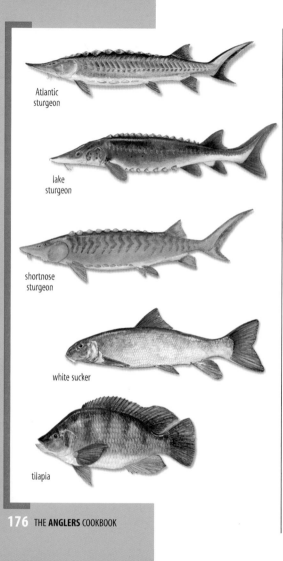

Atlantic
sturgeon

lake
sturgeon

shortnose
sturgeon

white sucker

tilapia

FRESHWATER FISH

STURGEON Few anglers ever see a sturgeon, despite the fact this great fish occurs in many parts of the country. When a sturgeon is caught in an area where it may be kept (sturgeon are fully protected in many places) it's usually cut into small pieces and smoked, but the flesh is quite good when fried, broiled, baked or used in a chowder. A sturgeon can be skinned, then filleted and the fillets cut into usable-size pieces; or the fish can be steaked.

SUCKER Several species of sucker are relished by many people in various parts of the country. The meat is sweet but bony. Preparing as for pickerel will help. Suckers are generally scaled and filleted, but sometimes have a muddy taste. If so, they should be filleted and skinned. Frying is the rule. Sucker meat is quite good when boiled, the bones picked out, and the flesh used for fish cakes or in recipes calling for flaked fish.

TILAPIA Although tilapia—members of the huge cichlid family of tropical climes around the world—are not native to North America, several varieties of them have become established around the country—most of them in Florida, although some species are highly opportunistic and have managed to overcome their tropical background and catch hold in various temperate waters. Considering the country as a whole, sports anglers are not responsible for putting very many tilapia on our tables. Most are the products of aquaculture and are sold either whole (panfish size) or as fillets. Regardless, they all have white flesh that is firm and very tasty, and that can be prepared in any way you like. Fried tilapia are especially good, but they don't lose a thing when sautéed, broiled, steamed or baked. Tilapia fillets are usually even firm enough to stand up well when cooked on the outside grill.

TROUT Almost all cold, unpolluted waters of North America hold trout of one kind or another—natural or introduced, native or hatchery-stocked. All are among the most prized of table fish, but there are definite levels of desirability—reminiscent of graded beef. To begin with, hatchery fish are lowest on the list. But unless you have a taste mechanism tuned to long years of getting your choice, don't let this bother you, because hatchery trout are delicious. It's just that natives are even more delicious. Naturally, there are preferences by species, too. And just as naturally, these preferences do vary among individuals. But it's a safe bet that the eastern trout fan will prefer brookies to rainbows or browns, while his western counterpart will take cutthroats or brookies over the same pair of game, but often snubbed, species. Readers who have their own ideas about eating trout likely won't be swayed by words printed here. As for the rest of you, be assured that you'll enjoy any trout that graces your table. As to handling and preparation, small trout should be slit and drawn, gills removed, and the fish pan fried, poached or baked. They can also be split and broiled. Remove the head if you prefer. Some trout grow large in big water. These include not only the sea-run rainbows called steelhead but also landlocked rainbows in large lakes and big rivers. Mammoth brown trout are sometimes caught, too. The Dolly Varden grows to huge size, as does the lake trout. If you're lucky enough to get one of those giants and don't prefer to hang it on the wall, it can be treated as for salmon.

WALLEYE With its white, fine-grained flesh and outstanding flavor, the walleye is a table favorite of anglers throughout the heartland. Although suitable for any form of cooking, it is probably most popular when filleted and fried.

WHITEFISH Great Lakes whitefish, lake cisco and mountain whitefish are related species that can be treated the same. All are excellent eating. Scale and prepare as for panfish, or scale and fillet, or split. Delicious and well known as smoked fish; whitefish also are good fried, broiled or baked.

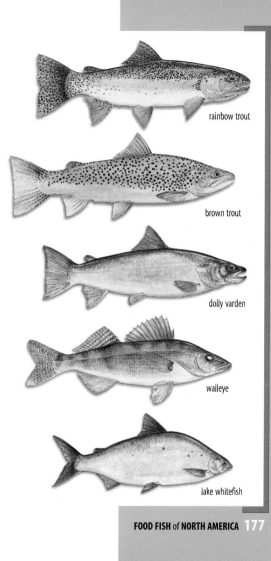

rainbow trout

brown trout

dolly varden

walleye

lake whitefish

SALTWATER FISH

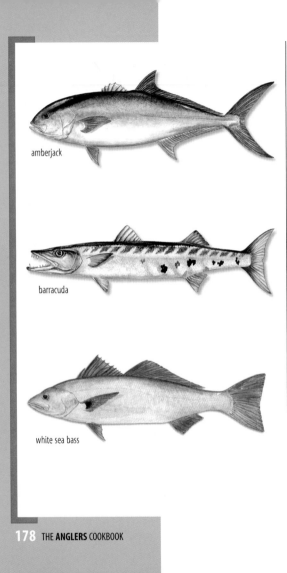

amberjack

barracuda

white sea bass

AMBERJACK This fish is very good, a fact which comparatively few anglers realized until recent years. Fillet the fish and skin the fillets, then "steak" each of the fillets into serving-size pieces. Trim off any red meat. Prepare any way you like, fried, broiled, chowdered, even baked in a sauce of some kind. You may find parasites in the flesh near the tail, but seldom in other areas. Cut out the infested portion and discard. Parasites are common in most species of fish, but noticeable in only a few, so don't let them bother you. In any event, they're completely harmless when the fish is cooked.

BARRACUDA There are several species of barracuda, of which the best known are the Pacific variety and the great barracuda of the South Atlantic and Caribbean. Both of those merit raves on the table, but care must be taken when eating the great barracuda, because they sometimes carry a toxin called ciguatera. There are quick tests to determine if a particular specimen might be so afflicted. The poison seems to be encountered only in larger fish from deep water, and only in certain tropical areas. Fish of five pounds or less, from the Florida flats or inshore waters, are safe and delicious. Ciguatera poisoning is rarely fatal, but is painful and lingering—so don't take chances by eating big barracuda. Pacific barracuda—the species so common off the California coast—is never poisonous. The great barracuda also occurs in the South Pacific, but not in California waters. Barracudas are easily filleted and skinned and this is by far the best way to prepare them. Any red meat may be trimmed away, although it doesn't seem to impair the taste. Fillets can be cooked any way you like. They are mild and lean.

BASS, WHITE SEA This is a potentially much larger Pacific relative of the Atlantic seatrouts and the various Pacific corvinas. The great fish lends itself to just about any type of cleaning or cooking. Fish of appropriate size may be scaled and prepared for baking. They can be filleted and skinned, and with the big ones it's best to do it this way. Few fish are better when fried, but you can cook them any way you prefer. The meat is mild, but flavorful and white.

BASS, CALIFORNIA BLACK This huge fish is much like the goliath grouper, (formerly called jewfish) and other very large groupers. Like most of our remaining giant fishes, it is no longer abundant and, in fact, the fishery is closed in California.

BASS, SEA The common sea bass is also called black bass or blackfish in certain areas of the Atlantic and Gulf coasts. Most of them are small, but these are one of the sweetest of all panfish. Scale and dress as for other panfish. Some are large enough to skin and fillet, or even to bake. The meat is fine-grained and white, a superb table fish.

BASS, KELP Along with the rock bass and sand bass, which are closely related and often confused, the kelp bass is a good food fish of the California coast. Prepare whole for baking, or fillet and skin for frying or broiling.

BLUEFISH Delicious but very rich and oily, the bluefish should be put on ice immediately and eaten as soon as possible after it has left the water. They're best the first day, but can be kept several days if well iced and kept drained. Small "snapper blues" are marvelous panfish, dressed and pan-fried. Larger ones can be filleted "butterfly fashion" as described in Chapter 10, and the fillets stuffed and baked. Or fillets can be cut singly, without scaling or skinning, and broiled. Skinned fillets are good fried. Whole blues of appropriate size can be dressed and baked.

BONEFISH Sportsmen rightly hold that bonefish should be released instead of eaten. But if a bonefish is inadvertently killed it can make a fine dinner. The only problem is— you guessed it—bones. Fillet the bonefish butterfly fashion (see Chapter 10). Broil the double fillet, skin side down. When done, a great many bones will "arch up" from the meat. Pick these away carefully and then dig in—but cautiously, because more bones remain in the flesh. The flesh, though, is fat and quite tasty, and needs nothing more than some salt and lemon.

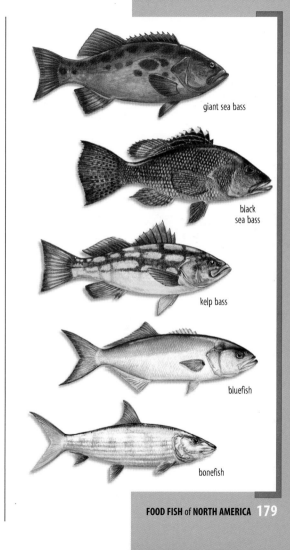

giant sea bass

black sea bass

kelp bass

bluefish

bonefish

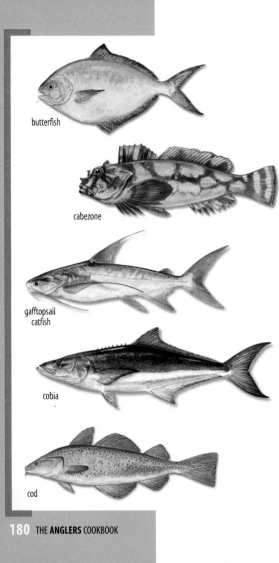

butterfish

cabezone

gafftopsail
catfish

cobia

cod

SALTWATER FISH

BUTTERFISH This is a generally large panfish, which can be scaled and dressed whole for baking, or scaled and filleted for frying or broiling. Very tasty.

CABEZONE One of the largest members of the sculpin family, the Pacific cabezone is best when filleted and skinned. Though not much for looks, the fish is quite good eating.

CATFISH Unlike their freshwater relatives, saltwater catfish are not highly prized as table fare. The common sea catfish is edible but not popular. The gafftopsail catfish is bigger, gamer, and has the reputation of being better to eat as well—having pinkish flesh that is good fried, and great in chowders or stews. Unfortunately, the gafftopsail is covered with a thick slime that makes skinning a distasteful chore. Skin saltwater catfish the same way as freshwater catfish.

COBIA By whatever name it's known (often called ling or lemonfish), the cobia is an unusual and excellent food fish—unusual because most agree it "doesn't taste like fish." The flavor has been likened to chicken or frog legs. Cobia have thick, shark-like skin. They should be filleted and skinned. Large fish can be skinned first, then filleted, and the fillets cut into steaks. Or they can be steaked without filleting. In small pieces, cobia is delicious fried. Large chunks and steaks can be broiled or baked. The meat is dry, so use sauce or butter while cooking.

COD Little need be said about the table qualities of the cod. Most caught these days are smallish and best filleted, either with or without skinning. Butterfly fillets, with skin left on, are the kind you see for salted cod. Salt cod is a staple in many parts of the world, but fresh cod is out of this world. Broil, bake, chowder or cake, you can hardly find a bad way to cook fresh cod, the meat of which is mild, white and fine-grained.

CORVINA (CORBINA) This name is applied to various members of the weakfish or seatrout genus of Pacific waters, and also to the California corvina, which is of the same family but more closely resembles the croakers. Regardless, they are all among the best table fish of the Pacific, and prime favorites throughout the tropical Americas. The meat is mild and white. Scale and prepare whole for baking; scale and fillet, or fillet and skin. Suit yourself. And cook any way you like. Corvina is the fish usually chosen in Latin America for making seviche (see Chapter 9).

CROAKER Many types of croaker are found along the Atlantic, Pacific and Gulf coasts. All are very good. Usually pan-size, they should be scaled and dressed whole. Sometimes, however, they reach two pounds or more and can be dressed whole for baking, or filleted. They're excellent fried, baked or broiled.

DRUM, BLACK When small—around five pounds or less—black drum are surprisingly good, especially if filleted, skinned and fried. Up to perhaps 10 pounds they are good scaled, dressed and baked. Let the giant ones go; they're often full of parasites.

DRUM, RED Also called redfish and channel bass, among other names, this is a popular food fish and a very good one in small sizes. Reds up to seven or eight pounds can be filleted and skinned, then fried, broiled, boiled or baked. Up to 12 pounds or so, they are still fine for baking, and for this they should be scaled, drawn and beheaded. Trophy-sized reds are outrageously coarse-fleshed, and if eaten at all, should be used in chowder or ground for cakes. Large red drum are now fully protected in many jurisdictions.

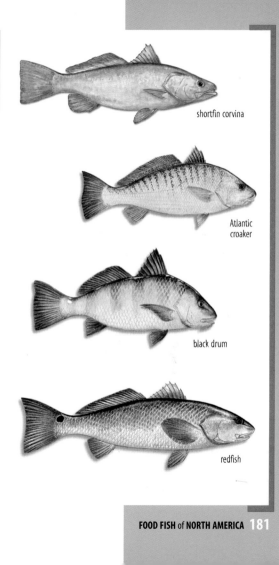

shortfin corvina

Atlantic croaker

black drum

redfish

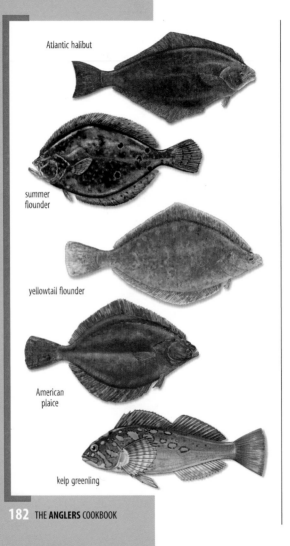

Atlantic halibut

summer flounder

yellowtail flounder

American plaice

kelp greenling

SALTWATER FISH

FLATFISH Lumped together in this category are all the "doormats," those strange-looking but invariably excellent tasting fish which are flat and have both eyes on the same (upper) side. Included are the giant halibuts of Atlantic and Pacific, the small dabs, the flounders, flukes and soles. Names are often confused. Several kinds are often represented as "sole" on restaurant menus, and seldom if ever is a customer the wiser. The rib cavity, encompassing the entrails, is quite small on all flatfish. To clean, simply cut off the head, make a small slit below and remove the entrails. Some cooks prefer to leave the head on, in which case the gills should be removed. Scales on most flatfish are relatively small, though large enough on bigger fish to warrant scaling. Seldom is a flatfish skinned. Small specimens can be left whole after cleaning, and then can be fried, broiled, baked or pan-fried. Very large fish—halibut and the occasional huge fluke—can be steaked. Big specimens of any flatfish can be filleted with a long knife, and the fillets cut into suitable pieces for broiling, frying, or for baking with a stuffing.

GREENLING Several varities of greenling are found off the Pacfic Coast of North America from about the middle of California northward to Alaska. Their name owes to the fact that their flesh is green, but you shouldn't let that toss you for a loop. While cooking, the meat turns white and flaky, and is ranked among the best. Greenling should be filleted and skined, then fried or baked. The Pacific lingcod is closely related, and, in fact may itself be a greenling. Biologists are divided on this, but it can at least be said that the lingcod makes just as good table fare as the (other?) greenlings and is generally much larger.

GROUPER The groupers are a big clan, covering tropical and subtropical waters of both oceans and the Gulf of Mexico. They encompass many species, from warsaw to the huge goliath grouper (now protected), to tiny coneys. Those of primary interest to anglers—both as prey and table fare—fall into two main groupings, or genera, as follows. Genus *Mycteroperca*, represented in the South Atlantic and Gulf by such species as the black, yellowfin, gag and scamp, and in Lower California by such types as the golden and broomtail. Members of this bunch are rather streamlined, as groupers go and, more important for our immediate purposes, somewhat better eating—being finer grained. Genus *Epinephelus* is represented in the Atlantic by such groupers as the red, Nassau and the hinds, and in Mexican Pacific waters by the cabrillas. These are less streamlined, more potbellied than the above group and of coarser flesh. All groupers are usually filleted and skinned, although it's quite all right to draw and prepare them whole for baking. In that case, there is no need to scale, since the tough skin will not be eaten anyway. Smaller groupers of any kind provide fillets which are excellent when fried. Large groupers are also quite good for frying if the fillets are sliced rather thin. All types are great for chowders and stews, while large fillets, or chunks of large fillets, are excellent if baked in a sauce.

GRUNT These are among the best of saltwater panfish, preferred by many old-time Floridians to snapper. Scale and prepare them whole for pan-frying. If unusually large, grunts may be scaled and filleted, or even baked whole. There are numerous species, differing in appearance, but not taste. However, the largest of all—the white margate grunt, which can reach a weight of 15 pounds—tastes very strong when freshly caught, but loses the strong taste after a day or two on ice or a short period of freezing.

HADDOCK Closely related to the cod, and similar in appearance, haddock may be treated in the same way.

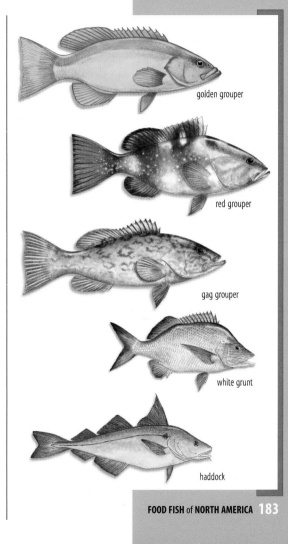

golden grouper

red grouper

gag grouper

white grunt

haddock

SALTWATER FISH

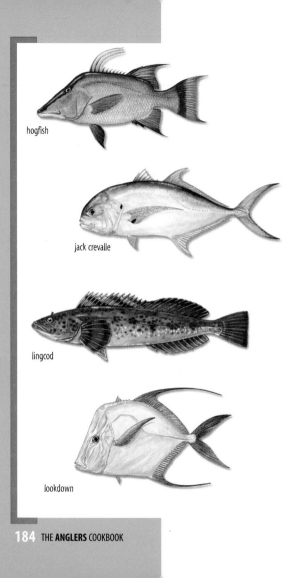

hogfish

jack crevalle

lingcod

lookdown

HOGFISH Sometimes called hog snapper, though it is not a snapper but a wrasse, the hogfish is thought by many to be the finest tasting fish of South Atlantic reefs. Certainly, it would be hard to imagine fish flesh any more fine-grained or pure white. Fillet and skin, then fry, broil or boil. When boiled and served with a bit of salt and melted butter, it tastes much like crab or lobster.

JACK Incredibly, all the jacks have long had the reputation of being very poor table fare—in the States, at least. Actually, they are among the very best of fish, a fact which isn't yet widely known or accepted. They do require a bit of extra cleaning effort, but not much. After being filleted and skinned, the fillets should be cut in half, lengthwise, and the red meat running the length of each piece should be carefully trimmed away—along with some extra bones that lie along that center line. Trimmed fillets may be fried, broiled or boiled for salad. Delicious! These directions apply to all the jacks, including the jack crevalle, blue runner, bar jack and almaco or Spanish jack. Perhaps the bar jack is a shade tastier than the others.

LINGCOD The lingcod is a great sportfishing favorite and can grow quite large, perhaps as big as a hundred pounds. Like the related greenlings, it is a popular food fish. It should be filleted and skinned, after which it is suitable for all types of preparation. The greenish flesh of the lingcod is disconcerting but not harmful. It whitens upon cooking.

LOOKDOWN Excellent eating and easy to clean. Cut off head and remove entrails, which are in a small pocket just below the gills. Pan-fry or bake the whole fish—or chop in half if you get one too big for your pan. One of the best panfish, the lookdown is similar in flavor to its relative, the pompano.

MACKEREL Several mackerel species in the Atlantic and Pacific are similar in table quality. All have oily flesh good for broiling, smoking or salting. Mackerel need not be scaled or skinned. Simply slice off the fillets and broil—or else cut the fillets butterfly-fashion (see Chapter 10) for smoking. Largest is king mackerel, frequently called kingfish, or king. These are steaked, rather than filleted, though small specimens can be filleted. Kings of 20 pounds and larger carry a health advisory, because of mercury buildup. Other mackerel species, cero and the sierra, are tasty and sometimes grow large enough to steak.

MAHI-MAHI Called dolphin by most offshore anglers, this deepwater fish occurs around the world and is a choice table variety everywhere. The fillets are at their best when baked or broiled, but are also good fried. Keep dolphin well iced, as they grow soft quickly.

MARGATE The white margate of Florida reefs looks exactly like a huge grunt, which indeed it is. The black margate belongs to the same family but is not thought of as a grunt because of its large size and dissimilar appearance. The black margate can be scaled and prepared whole for baking, or it can be filleted and skinned for frying or broiling.

MARLIN These great gamefish of the deep oceans come in several varieties and all should be released. However, when one is landed dead are brought to the dock, it is usually smoked—a real treat. Steaks from marlin are good broiled or baked, but not nearly so good as to influence the deliberate killing of one of these great fish.

MULLET The mullet is one of the tastiest fish in Florida—very rich and buttery. Eat it soon after catching. Because of the oily flesh, poorly kept mullet become rancid quickly. Scale and fillet, then fry or broil. It's also excellent when smoked or salted, and the large roe is marvelous. Many mullet are caught by hook-and-line anglers in freshwater rivers, where they are "muddy" tasting. To remove the muddy taste, fillet and skin.

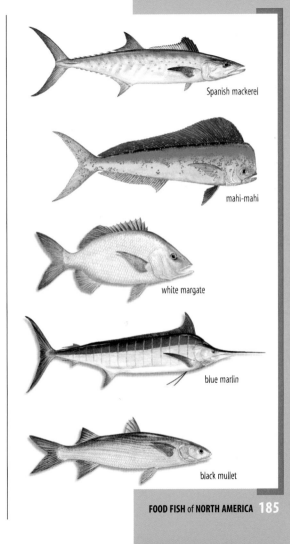

Spanish mackerel

mahi-mahi

white margate

blue marlin

black mullet

white perch

permit

pollock

pompano

SALTWATER FISH

PERCH This name is incorrectly but widely applied to quite a few smallish saltwater fish—especially to several related types of surf or sea perches common everywhere along the Pacific Coast. In the Atlantic, there is the sand perch of southern waters. One true perch of the Atlantic is the white perch, caught in both salt water and in freshwater streams. There's no need to try separating all these biologically. If a fish wears the name "perch" you can be sure it is an excellent panfish. Scale and prepare whole for pan-frying. Some types do exceed panfish size and can be filleted and skinned or scaled. Usually deep-fried, perch fillets are also good broiled or used in chowder.

PERMIT When small—under seven pounds—it takes a fin-count to distinguish a permit from the common pompano. A cook or gourmet couldn't tell the difference. See the listing for pompano. Large permit—they grow commonly to 30 pounds, and sometimes twice that weight—are also a table treat. Sportsmen play down their appeal in hopes that most folks will release the big ones. A big permit should be filleted and skinned. Next, the fillets should be trimmed of dark meat, then sliced into pieces about the size of minute steaks. And then comes the surprise. Those pieces of permit will taste like the best veal, but of course are much whiter.

POLLOCK Strangely, the pollock is not highly regarded as a food fish by anglers, although it is similar to cod in both appearance and taste. The flesh is not nearly so fine-grained as the cod, and this could be a contributing reason. Still, pollock is quite good when filleted and sliced thin for frying or broiling.

POMPANO According to price, pompano is the best fish in the sea, usually served up in fancy dishes. But there's really no need to get fancy. Small pompano, sautéed in a pan, and larger ones baked or broiled can stand on their own as sheer delights—without help from fancy sauces. You needn't scale or skin the fish; simply cut off the head and draw. Fillet, if you prefer. There are several species of pompano, and all are superb.

PORGY/SHEEPSHEAD Here's another panfish favorite that comes in several varieties and often runs large enough to provide sizeable fillets. Whether to scale or to skin is a personal option. Skinning is much easier. Fried fingers are delicious.

PUFFER This heading covers the blowfish or swellfish, and also the rabbitfish or silver puffer. Proceed with caution, however. All are among the very tastiest fish, having a flavor similar to frog legs and, when marketed commercially in the northeastern states, are frequently labeled "sea chicken." However, certain internal organs of some species of puffer can be very poisonous. Apparently there is nothing to fear from the northern variety of blowfish since, as mentioned, huge quantities of them are consumed. Many people in Florida also relish the southern blowfish and rabbitfish, and cases of poisoning are rare, though they can be fatal. For that reason, puffers are protected from harvest in Florida.

RAINBOW RUNNER A deepwater member of the jack family, this fish is excellent when skinned and trimmed of red meat. Fry or broil.

RAYS The danger with rays is not in eating them, but in handling. Many have dangerous barbed spikes in the tail. Some can administer an electric shock. Obviously, fishermen don't often bring them home—but the "wings" are very good to eat. A good way to handle rays or skates is to cut off both wings. A layer of cartilage is located in the center of each wing, so you must slice fillets off above and below this cartilage—the same as slicing two fillets away from the backbone of other fishes. Finally, you skin the fillets in the normal manner. Chunks cut from the wings resemble scallops in flavor.

ROCKFISH Pacific Coast rockfish species are many, varied—and delicious. Probably more than half the sportsmen's catch in California salt water is made up of rockfish of one species or another. Fillet and skin, and then prepare in any way you prefer. This name is also used for grouper in the Bahamas. See the listing for grouper.

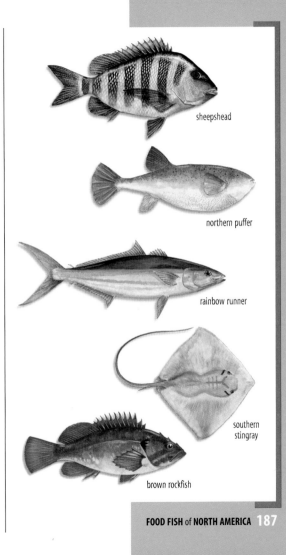

sheepshead

northern puffer

rainbow runner

southern stingray

brown rockfish

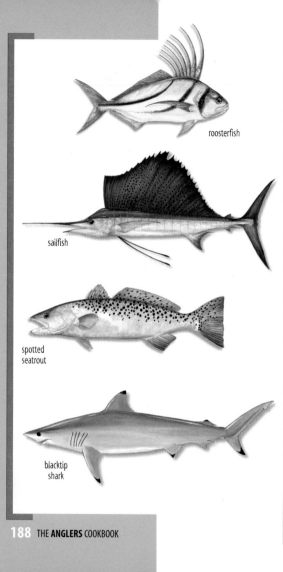

roosterfish

sailfish

spotted
seatrout

blacktip
shark

SALTWATER FISH

ROOSTERFISH Like the jacks, which are close relatives, the roosterfish of Lower California should be filleted and skinned, and trimmed of dark meat. Also like the jack, it's seldom chosen for the table, but the smaller ones are quite good.

SAILFISH Here's another species that is far more valuable in the water than on the table. But if you bring in a sailfish, for whatever reason, by all means smoke it or have it smoked commercially. Its fillets can be broiled or grilled into good fare, but not so well as many other varieties of fish that are not so heavily pressured.

SEATROUT Members of this group are also referred to as weakfishes. The Atlantic seatrouts, of which the spotted or speckled trout and the northern or common weakfish are the most prominent, are brothers to the Pacific corvinas and the California white sea bass. Outstanding food fish, they are usually scaled and drawn. Then they can be either filleted or left whole for baking. Along the Gulf coast, those of barely legal size are frequently dressed whole and served individually, either baked or pan-fried. Usually the head is left on, but this is optional.

SHARK Most sharks are edible, and some highly prized. Steaks cut from the mako shark sometimes masquerade as swordfish steaks. The common nurse shark of the South is also a good dinner—again, steaked and broiled. The dogfish, a small shark of northern waters, is the original "fish and chips" and still the best, say British fans—so good that the species has been seriously overfished and substitutes are now the rule. Blacktip, leopard, lemon and other common shark varieties all make good table fare, though tiger and hammerhead are low on the list. Because of their tough skin, sharks are difficult to dress, but anglers generally keep only the smaller specimens and these can be handled with patience and good tools. Simply fillet and skin as with softer-skinned fish. All sharks can develop a very disagreeable odor due to uric acid in the flesh and especially the skin, and this turns many fishermen away from trying them. The odor, however, is easily combated. It probably will disappear after the meat has been iced for a few hours, or after it has been frozen for a while. If any lingering odor remains, it can be taken care of by soaking the flesh in lightly salted water for about an hour. Shark meat is firm, white and mild and suitable for any recipe you might care to try.

SHEEPSHEAD, CALIFORNIA A very delicious fish with flaky white flesh. It should be skinned and filleted. Cook it any way you like, but when boiled and served either hot or cold, it tastes much like lobster.

SNAPPER The name is commonly given to small bluefish—see that listing. But rightfully the name belongs to a large family of exceptionally fine sport and food fish of the southern Atlantic, southern Pacific and Gulf waters. Best known in the marketplace is the red snapper. Among many others are (Atlantic) the mutton, lane, mangrove, schoolmaster, cubera and yellowtail; and (Lower California) striped, Colorado, rose, mullet and yellow snappers. The collective Spanish name is "pargo." While numerous personal preferences are expressed, all snappers, without exception, are marvelous table fish. Small ones, scaled and prepared whole, can be pan-fried or baked as individual servings. Larger ones are most easily filleted and skinned, unless you wish to bake the whole fish, which is a tasty idea. In that case, scale and draw it and cut off the head. Bake it stuffed or unstuffed. Even the biggest snappers, such as the cubera, are delicious and tender. Skin the giants and cut the meat into slices or large chunks for baking. Cubera and dog snappers have been implicated in ciguatera poisoning, however. Eating bigger examples of both species from around coral reefs is taking a chance, unless a sample of the fish can be tested.

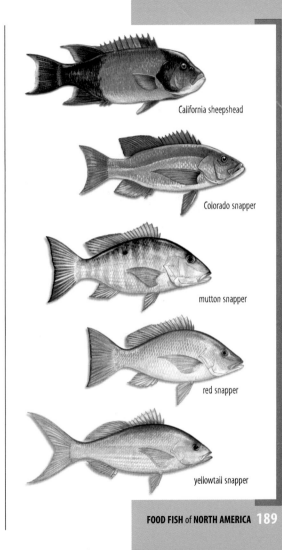

California sheepshead

Colorado snapper

mutton snapper

red snapper

yellowtail snapper

SALTWATER FISH

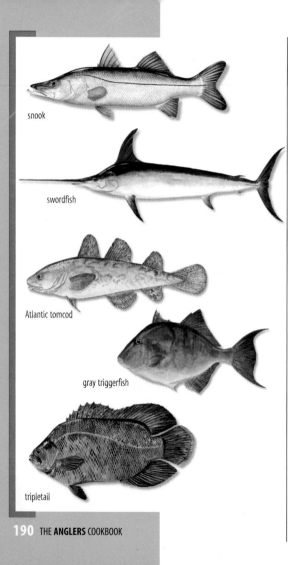

snook

swordfish

Atlantic tomcod

gray triggerfish

tripletail

SNOOK This is one of the best southern fish. It yields very thick fillets and should *always* be filleted and skinned. Without skinning, it has a soapy taste. Slice the fillets into small pieces, or "fingers," and deep-fry. It is also good broiled or baked, or used in chowder.

SWORDFISH The steaks are justly famous, but its popularity as a food fish has caused stocks to diminish to a critical level. Sportsmen are no longer as likely to land a swordfish, but any who do can fillet the fish (a big job!) and cut steaks from the fillets. Suitable for any number of preparations, swordfish steaks are at their best when grilled or broiled and served with your choice of mild sauces.

TOMCOD Though not as highly regarded as its larger relative the cod, the tomcod is just about as good on the table and can be treated in the same ways—which means just bout any way the cook can wish. The meat is very white and mild. The biggest difference, of course, is size. Tom cod are always small—smaller even than the junior-size codfish which are listed on menus as "scrod."

TRIGGERFISH The several varieties of triggerfish, including the common gray, the beautiful queen trigger and the large ocean tally (sometimes called turbot), are very good and preferred by some over snapper. They are, however, tough to clean because of a very leathery skin. They can be filleted and then skinned, but require a strong, sharp knife. The fillets are quite delicious either deep-fried or broiled.

TRIPLETAIL Odd-looking but fine-eating, the tripletail is best when filleted and skinned, after which it can be cut into fingers and fried. It is also excellent when baked or broiled, although the flesh is lean and will require some basting.

TUNA Americans, whether they catch their tuna or buy them in cans, almost invariably express their preferences in terms of the lightest, prettiest meat. Thus the "finest" tuna is the white-meat albacore of the Pacific, and the "worst" are the little tunny and other dark-meat "bonitos," which all too many anglers regard as inedible. Actually, however, the dark tunas are the most nutritious and are the preferred species in some parts of the world. Any of the tunas, including the blackfin, are scrumptious when boiled and made into salad, or pan-broiled in thin slices with butter and seasonings. Of course, thicker tuna steaks, usually yellowfin, are often grilled and, when served in fine restaurants, draw high praise from customers. Raw slivers of bluefin and yellowfin tuna are among the most coveted fish by lovers of sushi and sashimi, who are willing to pay exorbitant prices.

WAHOO This is an excellent offshore game and food fish, similar in appearance to the king mackerel, though with whiter meat and less oily flavor. Best when steaked and broiled, it is also a great fish for smoking.

WHITING These are small, slender fish of croaker-like appearance. They're most often scaled, drawn and beheaded, then pan-fried. The flesh is soft. Whiting should be used immediately after catching. They're also called "kingfish" or "king whiting."

YELLOWTAIL, ATLANTIC See Snapper.

YELLOWTAIL, PACIFIC A California favorite, yellowtail are a type of amberjack. They can be either filleted and skinned, or steaked. They're delicious fried, broiled—or just about any way you care to prepare them.

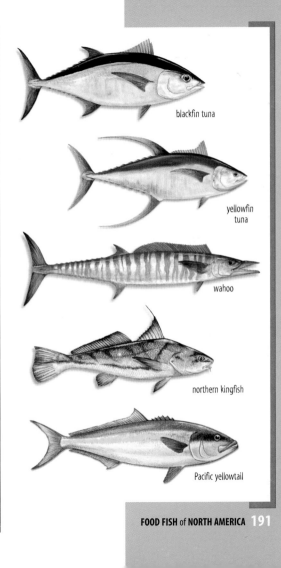

blackfin tuna

yellowfin tuna

wahoo

northern kingfish

Pacific yellowtail

APPENDIX
FISH FOR YOUR HEALTH

Unlike many other "diet" foods, fish is both healthful *and* enjoyable. It provides a great deal of high-quality protein with little fat. And if you happen to be one of millions who are on a low-carbohydrate diet, take note that all but a few species of fish are totally devoid of carbs, while the rest contain barely a trace. And when it comes to comparing the ratio of calories to protein, fish is a clear and overwhelming winner. Ground beef delivers about 18 percent protein, about the same amount as a similar serving of the most popular fish. But an 8-ounce hamburger patty, made from regular ground beef, contains 640 calories, while fish has a mere 200 to 300, depending on the species.

The benefits of a high-fish diet don't end there. It has long been proven that eating fish regularly leads to better health and longevity. Omega-3 fatty acid, the special ingredient proven to prevent cancer, that lowers the risk of heart disease and helps cure mental ailments and much more, is found to some extent in all fish. It's concentrated at the most health-giving levels in those fish species that have dark and/or oily flesh. These include tuna, herring, trout and salmon.

A study by the Center for Genetics, Nutrition and Health in Washington D.C. reported that Omega-3 polyunsaturated fatty acids are essential for human health, but that their intake has gradually declined over the years. During most of mankind's evolution, the ratio of healthy Omega 3 to unhealthy Omega 6 fatty acids was thought to be 1:1, but today the ratio is at least 10:1, and often higher, in favor of the bad stuff.

The study concludes that we should all eat more fish, a recommendation that is heartily seconded here, and suggests that all of us take fish-oil supplements as well.

Unfortunately, some types of fish in certain areas may also harbor substances that are potentially *unhealthy*. These are man-made pollutants that pose a health risk to particular individuals, or possibly even to anyone who overindulges. It always pays to check for any health advisories that affect the fish you may catch in your local waters. Such advisories are in effect for many kinds of fish nationwide, and most often they merely offer recommendations as to how much one should eat of certain species, and how often.

The following table gives basic nutritional information for many popular food fish of both fresh and salt water.

SPECIES (3 oz. fillet)	CALORIES	PROTEIN (grams)	TOTAL FAT (grams)
Bass, *fresh water*	90	15	2.9
Bass, Black Sea	100	20	2.0
Bass, Striped	110	19	3.0
Bluefish	130	21	5.0
Catfish	120	19	6.4
Cod	90	19	1.0
Flounder	100	20	1.5
Haddock	90	20	1.0
Halibut	120	22	2.5
Herring	170	19	10.0
Mackerel	190	21	12.0
Mahi Mahi	90	20	1.0
Pike, Northern	75	16	1.0
Porgy	120	21	3.0

SPECIES	CALORIES	PROTEIN	TOTAL FAT
Rockfish	100	20	3.0
Salmon, Atlantic	150	22	7.0
Salmon, Coho	150	22	7.0
Salmon, King	200	22	11.5
Seatrout	120	18	5.0
Shark	140	22	5.0
Smelt	100	19	2.0
Sturgeon	89	14	3.4
Tilapia	85	18	1.0
Trout, *fresh water*	130	22	4.0
Tuna, Yellowfin	120	25	4.6
Walleye	90	19	1.0
Whitefish	140	20	6.0
Whiting	100	19	1.0

INDEX

INDEX

INDEX

INDEX

ADD YOUR FAVORITES

INGREDIENTS

INGREDIENTS

ADD YOUR
FAVORITES

INGREDIENTS

   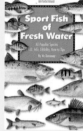